OUR DIFFERENT GIFTS

BERNADETTE STANKARD

OUR DIFFERENT GIFTS

A **catechist's guide** to
using **multiple intelligences**
in **faith formation**

TWENTY
THIRD 23rd
PUBLICATIONS
NEW LONDON, CT 06320
WWW.23RDPUBLICATIONS.COM

ACKNOWLEDGMENTS

Poem on page 40 from Daniel Ladinsky.
The Gift. Daniel Ladinsky, translator.
Penguin Group Inc., Copyright 1999.
Used with permission.

Poem on page 82 from Daniel Ladinsky.
Love Poems from God. Daniel Ladinsky,
translator. Penguin Group Inc. Copyright
2002. Used with permission.

TWENTY-THIRD PUBLICATIONS
A Division of Bayard
One Montauk Avenue, Suite 200
New London, CT 06320
(860) 437-3012 or (800) 321-0411
www.23rdpublications.com

Cover image ©iStockphoto.com/Antagain

ISBN 978-1-58595-912-9
Library of Congress Control Number: 2013932059

Printed in the U.S.A.

TABLE OF CONTENTS

MULTIPLE INTELLIGENCES

Verbal-Linguistic Intelligence: Well-developed verbal skills and sensitivity to the sounds, meanings, and rhythms of words.

Logical-Mathematical Intelligence: Ability to think conceptually and abstractly with the capacity to discern logical or numerical patterns.

Musical-Rhythmic Intelligence: Ability to produce and appreciate rhythm, pitch, and timbre.

Visual-Spatial Intelligence: Capacity to think in images and pictures and to visualize accurately and abstractly.

Bodily-Kinesthetic Intelligence: Ability to control one's body movements and to handle objects skillfully.

Interpersonal Intelligence: Capacity to detect and respond appropriately to the moods, motivations, and desires of others.

Intrapersonal Intelligence: Capacity to be self-aware and in tune with one's inner feelings, values, beliefs, and thinking process.

Naturalist Intelligence: Ability to sense patterns in, and to make connections to, elements in nature.

Existential Intelligence: Sensitivity and capacity to tackle deep questions about human existence, such as the meaning of life, why do we die, and how did we get here.

ONE

JESUS THE GREAT TEACHER

*Howard Gardner's theory of multiple intelligences
postulates that there are many actual intelligences.
When we teach to these intelligences, we know that
a great depth of faith development takes place.*

■ **B. CUDNIK**, TEACHER

J esus wouldn't pass today's requirements for teaching. He would fail miserably on paperwork, probably rebel against grading, and wouldn't stay on the curriculum requirements. As far as "no child left behind," he would rework that to read "no one person left behind." Yet, because of his methods, Jesus would be one of the most sought-after, talked-about, complained-about teachers alive today, because Jesus is someone who embodies all the elements of the theory of multiple intelligences. He was practicing the theory ages before it was first brought up by Howard Gardner of Harvard University.

Jesus, a Jewish man in a small country called Palestine, traveled the length and breadth of the area, talking with people and reaching all those who were open to his words. To make sure that all people understood him, he addressed them in what today we would call their individual intelligences.

When asked about how Jesus taught, many of us would quickly point out the parables. He taught many of life's great lessons in simple terms people could understand. He drew from the scenarios they knew and could relate to. For instance, people of his day understood what it

was to have a crop fail. They felt the pain of someone who was neglect-
ed by the rich, while a foreign Samaritan could be the embodiment of
kindness. Storytelling was definitely Jesus' forte. Through that medium
he was able to reach many people who had a strong verbal-linguistic
intelligence.

Also at that time, many people, because of the storytelling tradition, had a well-developed visual-spatial intelligence—being able to
translate an abstract story heard by the ears to a vibrant story alive in
the mind's eye.

However, Jesus didn't ignore those people who carried the logical-
mathematical intelligence. The multiplication of the loaves and fishes
must have driven the strong logical-mathematical intelligences mad as
they fought to logically understand how so many people were fed from
so few loaves and fishes.

In the Sermon on the Mount, Jesus happily engaged the musical-
rhythmic people through words: "Happy are those who know they are
spiritually poor; the Kingdom of heaven belongs to them! Happy are
those who mourn; God will comfort them! Happy are the meek; they
will receive what God has promised" (Matthew 5:3-5). As the words
went on, the people with musical-rhythmic intelligence must have felt
their hearts leap with joy, feeling the power of the words in the musical
way in which they were delivered.

For those who needed real hands-on occurrences to understand
fully, Jesus often used practical items. The mud placed on the blind
man's eyes, the cleansing of the temple, the walking on water, the tears
he shed as he looked out over Jerusalem—all these bodily-kinesthetic
actions touched those strong in that intelligence, bringing Jesus' message home for some of them.

There were two intelligences that Jesus addressed regularly because
of his own need. Often in Scripture, we read of Jesus going off alone to
pray to his Father. We read of him taking time away from the crowds—
and even the apostles—to be alone. These were the moments when he
could remember his calling, remember what he was about, and be in
touch with his Father. And by his doing so, he showed the people with

intrapersonal intelligence what was important for them to remember. Reflection, meditation, and other moments of quiet were important for a healthy person to grow. Otherwise, they would never come to know who they really were—children of his Father.

On the flip side, Jesus took time regularly to be with people. Mary, Martha, and Lazarus were good friends whom he often visited so he could relax as well as talk with them about the Father. He visited Peter's mother-in-law, his own mother, the Pharisees, and others, both to draw strength and to remember his mission. He was energized by people, and that is perhaps best demonstrated in the Scripture passage when he says, "'Let the little children come to me and do not stop them, because the Kingdom of God belongs to such as these. Remember this! Whoever does not receive the Kingdom of God like a child will never enter.' Then he took the children in his arms, placed his hands on each of them and blessed them" (Mark 10:13-16). And for the people with interpersonal intelligence around him, Jesus probably played with the children, demonstrating the importance of interpersonal activity.

During his preaching, Jesus often made references to the natural world, talking of sowing seeds, of fig trees not bearing fruit, of faith the size of mustard seeds, of studying trees and the fruit they bear. People with naturalist intelligence were touched by these references, and the words Jesus spoke often pointed out how God took care of every bit of creation, including us: "Look at the birds flying around: they do not plant seeds, gather a harvest, and put it in barns; your Father in heaven takes care of them. Aren't you worth much more than birds?" (Matthew 6:26).

Jesus knew that there were people in the crowds whose minds were trying to figure out how what he had to say fit into what they had been taught, what they believed. These people, with a strong existential intelligence, needed to struggle with the questions that Jesus' words awoke in them.

They probably pondered much over many of Jesus' words. When he said, "I am the real vine and my Father is the gardener. He breaks off every branch in me that does not bear fruit and prunes every branch that does bear fruit so that it will be clean and bear more fruit. You have been made clean already by the message I have spoken to you. Remain united to me and I will remain united to you....Whoever remains in me and I in him will bear much fruit, for you can do nothing without me" (John 15:1-5), they wondered about what this was saying to them and what they believed. What did it say for the world? The existential intelligence, then as now, struggles with the big questions.

Jesus, the teacher, reached many individuals with his teaching by addressing the whole person, by touching the strength within that person so that the heart would be able to learn.

Many years later, the theory of multiple intelligences came to the forefront when Howard Gardner, a professor at Harvard University, developed this educational approach for the modern world. He felt strongly that the traditional notion of intelligence, based on IQ testing, was very limiting and only addressed two of the intelligences—verbal-linguistic and logical-mathematical. Believing that intelligence was the ability to find and solve problems and create value in one's culture, Gardner started scientific research to determine ways in which people learn and use their unique gifts.

He concluded that there are many ways by which people know, understand, and learn about the world. Gardner emphasized that even though individuals often have one strong intelligence through which they first take in information, everyone has all the intelligences to some degree, and all the intelligences work together. This theory, rather than with the old theory of IQ, which excludes rather than includes, stresses the importance of learning from each other and making connections.

"In my own work," Gardner said in a 1999 interview with Stefanie Weiss from the National Education Association, "I'm a proponent of teaching for understanding, which means going deeply into topics so that students can really make use of knowledge in new situations. This is very, very different from most teaching, where people memorize material and can reproduce it on demand but can't make use of it in new situations. That's what understanding entails. If you favor education for understanding the way I do, then multiple intelligences can be extremely helpful. Because when you are teaching a topic you can approach the topic in many ways, thereby activating different intelligences."

How much of his theory applies to faith? If we believe God created each of us as unique, loving individuals with the ability to be creative, as our Creator is, then using the theory of multiple intelligences in religious education classrooms or faith formation gatherings ensures not only deeply unique encounters with God but also an awakening of the vast potential of each of us.

As Gardner points out, the goal of any education is creating the ability to enable the person to take what he or she has learned and apply it to various life situations. If the goal in religious education is understanding our faith, then we as a church must develop individuals who are thinking and caring souls, who take what they learn and apply it to everyday situations. This is the concept of a living faith, not a faith that is stagnant and unthinking.

Integrating multiple intelligences into the religious education classroom means taking a leap of faith and trusting the Spirit to guide you. In an earlier book, *How Each Child Learns: Using Multiple Intelligence in Faith Formation*, I spoke often of how many of the techniques used in integrating multiple intelligences into religious education are techniques that many of us are not comfortable with, having grown up with heavy emphasis on verbal-linguistic and logical-mathematical intelligences. When we move on to addressing other intelligences, we move into scary territory. We have to open ourselves up to not always being in control. We have to take a leap of faith and trust the Spirit to guide us.

One of the first times I used the theory in my classroom was in a preschool class of four- and five-year-olds. I had set up the classroom around the theme of baptism and belonging to a community of believers. There were places all around the room where the students could explore the different aspects of baptism. Even the baptismal font was wheeled in. After I explained the ceremony, those who wanted to conducted a baptism ceremony for their dolls. Others worked at tables studying water and what it could do to various fabrics and objects. Still others composed songs about welcome and belonging to a family. A few worked industriously at putting together stories of their own baptisms. One little boy worked alone, fashioning things out of clay, each creation different. After each was completed, he deposited it in a jar that he had requested at the start of class. I was going to ask him about what he was doing when another student asked for my attention. There was little time left when I finished, and I wanted to make sure we had time for a mystery tray; consequently, my encounter with Kyle never happened.

The mystery tray is something I have present in my religious education classroom, no matter the age of the students. It is a simple tray, usually decorated by the class at the beginning of the year. On it I place something that has a connection to our faith. Chosen beforehand and known only to me, this item is placed on the tray and covered so it is hidden, but its shape is visible. During the mystery tray time, the class can ask questions about its identity, to which I give yes or no answers; on really difficult items, I give hints. Once someone guesses what's on the tray, the object is revealed, and discussion follows about how it connects to what we believe about God, our community, our faith.

This particular time I had placed a baptismal candle on the tray and was ready to proceed with my planned teaching. That's when Kyle stepped in. He carried his jar over to me and said, "Can we use my jar as the mystery today?" I started to say no, but caught the look in his eyes and felt the tug of the Spirit at my heart.

"Okay," I replied, wondering what I was stepping into.

He turned to the kids gathered around our prayer altar and all ready for the mystery tray time. "We have a mystery jar today," he said, holding it high above his head. I instinctively reached out to catch it in case it started to fall. "What mystery is it holding?" he asked.

The kids rushed to gather around, each craning for a look at the jar's contents—the clay creations of Kyle—dropped into the jar throughout the class period.

"Candy?" guessed one little girl.

"No, silly, it's about baptism," Kyle said.

"It's what happens to water when it gets hard," piped up another. Kyle shook his head.

"It's what's left when that original stuff is washed away."

"It's the crud that collects at the bottom of the water thing."

"It's the Holy Spirit."

On and on went the guesses, all receiving a shake of Kyle's head. I touched Kyle's shoulder.

"It's time to let them know what the mystery is, Kyle."

"Okay." He held the jar out and unscrewed the top. He reached in for one of the clay creations. "This is Anna. She likes to sing." It was a musical note shaped crudely from the clay. Holding up another, he said, "This is David. He's strong." A snake with a hump sat on his hand. Arm muscles, I guessed.

And so it went one after another, each creation a talent of one of the kids in the class. Even I was included. A smile complete with teeth because I make the kids smile, Kyle said.

"What does this have to do with baptism, Kyle?" I wasn't sure if I would be able to handle the answer.

"When we're baptized, we're God's family. And families have different people." He held up the jar. "Baptism tells us to share all the things that make us special."

It was a simple but very profound revelation about the meaning of baptism through a small child who experienced the aspects of baptism and then was able to make the connections. It was made possible by addressing multiple intelligences in the classroom and allowing the Spirit to work, trusting that, at times, it was all right to relinquish control. The students were not only able to experience at their own rate and intelligence, but they were able, through their interaction, to begin to connect concepts of their faith in a way we often think is not possible for young children.

Many years have passed since that time, but even today I am continually struck by the way the Spirit works when I use multiple intelligences in any teaching situation, be it with children or adults. I have received similar comments from other teachers who applied some of the basic approaches used in *How Each Child Learns: Using Multiple Intelligence in Faith Formation.* They were amazed at some of the things happening in their classrooms, and many of them developed interesting ways to cultivate the intelligences in the weekly lesson.

Using multiple intelligences in the classroom carries many benefits. First, it allows both teacher and students to regard faith development more broadly. Dancing, singing the blues in prayer, figuring out the existence of God through mustard seeds, becoming a cross on Golgotha and explaining how the cross felt—all these activities are vital to growing in faith. They allow the unique spirit of each child to respond to their Creator in a personal way.

Not Just for Kids

Every person has multiple intelligences. We may have one or two particularly strong ones, but we have the capacity to develop all of the intelligences. Too often we think only of children when it comes to applying the theory, and we fail to realize that adults also would respond better if their particular intelligences were addressed. As educators, we also need to make greater use of multiple intelligences in our adult faith formation classes, urging these adults to greater heights in coming to know their God.

Second, addressing multiple intelligences allows God and faith to become a part of every aspect of a person's life. No longer will God be someone who is addressed only on Sunday and turned to only in need. Faith will become more holistic and no longer compartmentalized.

A third surprising response is often the greater participation of parents and other family members in activities, because the multiple intelligences religious education classroom is always open to teaching—teaching done by and with the children. Parents are often amazed to see their children expounding on aspects of faith that sometimes they haven't even considered.

Another result when we take the leap of faith into multiple intelligences is that community develops more easily and directly. Children call upon each other in the classroom time and share their strengths with one another. The students' "expertise" in different areas of faith is honored, and adult faith journeys are shared.

Finally, the greatest benefit is that children and adults begin to understand, to integrate their faith into real-world situations. They begin to see God as a Divine Wonder who calls them again and again to fall in love. And if we as catechists respond to Jesus, the Teacher who used multiple intelligences those many years ago on a hillside in Palestine, we're following the best example.

TWO

MULTIPLE INTELLIGENCES AND APPLICATION TO FAITH FORMATION

This extraordinary burgeoning awareness of human capability was delightfully reflected by changes in the rules of chess. Prior to the Renaissance, the queen moved only one square at a time; but as the perception of human horizons and potential expanded, she was granted the wide-ranging powers she maintains to this day.

■ **MICHAEL GELB,** INNOVATOR AND AUTHOR

W hen I was in third grade, I was under the impression that school was something that you went to; you did the worksheets, and then you passed on to the next grade, where you did the same. I had no concept that school was for learning new ideas or that school was to broaden your knowledge of existing material. I loved the idea of doing projects because it gave me an opportunity to do something different. Unfortunately, these projects were few and far between. When the annual testing came and I did well, the only alternative for the teacher to give my parents was to suggest skipping a grade, but since my brother had a bad experience with that, my parents were not about to allow their daughter to skip one grade, let alone the two the teacher was suggesting. I was stuck in a world of schooling that held little wonder, excitement, or challenge.

Schools have come a long way since then. There are more opportunities for enriched education, and projects are encompassing hands-on activities, music, and more. Still, we tend to label kids according to their magical intelligence number instead of their many intelligences.

Around 1905 the world's first intelligence test was developed by Alfred Binet of France. Originally, it was used to determine mental retardation, but during World War I it became a quick and easy way to determine capabilities of the large number of men who were entering the armed forces. At this same time, because so many of the recruits were functionally illiterate, tests were devised that required little if any reading. Usually these tests consisted of a series of pictures that told a story with various pieces missing. The test taker was to fill the holes with the correct piece. If one did fill in all the pieces correctly or nearly so, one was said to be of "high ability."

After the war, the Binet's test gained in popularity, and its original use was lost in the effort to rank students and identify those who were more capable. Almost overnight, the test became the national standard for determining intelligence. When the test was revised by Lewis Terman of Stanford University, the intelligence quotient, or IQ, came into being. Intelligence was given a quotient—the ratio of mental age to chronological age. Renamed the Stanford-Binet Test, it measured students, separating them into superior, above-average, average, and below-average groupings.

Around this same time, psychologist David Wechsler was developing intelligence tests for both children and adults. According to Wechsler, the normal distribution of intelligence test scores—a bell-shaped, symmetrical curve—puts the majority of people in the middle and a relative few at the high and low ends. His approach almost predetermines a person's performance and allows for very little deviation in behavior or accomplishment.

Today, almost all of American education is decided by a student's scores on a series of intelligence tests, from entry into school at the age of five to entry into a university. Many educators prefer this way and see it as an opportunity to measure not only the student's performance, but the school's as well.

With all the testing, however, there was very little, until recently, that could be done for the child who was determined to be "gifted." Up to the mid-seventies, skipping a grade was the only option open to most students. More recently, gifted programs have sprung up to offer enrichment to these students, to build on their giftedness. Indeed, a whole industry of "giftedness" has sprung up around these children identified by a test score.

This approach to education does address certain needs in children. It does well in helping to identify the needs of the mentally challenged and in uncovering gifts that might otherwise lie fallow. However, many parents and educators express concern that such tests measure only raw intelligence or only how well a child reacts to standardized testing. The tests measure what a student can do, but do nothing to measure a student's potential. And often in special gifted programs for those marked as "gifted," the program only serves to separate and create divisions, often creating intelligent snobs who see themselves as better than anyone else.

Gratefully, new approaches in education are emerging, and one of the most talked about is the theory of multiple intelligences.

In his first book, *Frames of Mind: The Theory of Multiple Intelligences*, Howard Gardner introduced the idea that the traditional notion of intelligence based on IQ testing was very limited. He pointed out that there are several ways in which individuals take in information, and even though they may take in information in a particular intelligence, they have the capability of developing all of the intelligences.

His theory comes from extensive research done on the brain, including interviews, tests, and research on hundreds of individuals. His study addressed stroke and accident victims, prodigies, autistic individuals, those with learning disabilities, idiot savants, and people from many cultures.

What came out of all this work was the conclusion that there is not one fixed, inborn trait that dominates all the skills, problem-solving strategies, and learning abilities people possess. Instead, intelligence is centered in many different areas of the brain. All these areas are inter-

connected—working independently and yet relying on each other—
and, most importantly, can be developed under the right conditions.

This theory shook up the educational system, which was used to
being able to "test" and "measure" intelligence in order to determine
who was smart and who wasn't. Instead, if they bought into Gardner's
theory, they needed to look at individuals, each having different ways
to learn and the potential for strengthening other intelligences. In
short, Gardner was telling the educational community that all people
were gifted and had the power to develop their gifts even more.

At present nine intelligences have been identified:

Verbal-Linguistic: sensitivity to the sounds, meanings, order,
and rhythm of words.

Logical-Mathematical: the capacity and sensitivity to spot
logical or numerical patterns and to handle long chains of reasoning.

Musical-Rhythmic: the ability to produce and appreciate
rhythm, pitch, timbre, and various forms of musical expression.

Visual-Spatial: the ability to perceive the visual world accurately and then recreate the experience through form, color,
shape, and texture.

Bodily-Kinesthetic: the ability to use the body to express
emotion and to learn by doing and involving the whole body.

Naturalist: sensitivity to all features of the natural world with
the ability to categorize.

Intrapersonal: the knowledge of the internal aspects of self in
areas such as feelings, emotional responses, and self-reflection,
and an intuitive sense about spiritual realities.

Interpersonal: ability to detect and respond appropriately to the moods, motivations, and desires of others.

Existential: the sensitivity and capacity to tackle profound questions of human existence.

As with everything in life, this approach has pluses and minuses. One very important minus—as viewed from the education world and many parents—is that these intelligences are difficult to measure. That is a definite drawback in our culture, which likes to know where everyone stands. What has been learned cannot be quantified. "How do we know the children know the material?" we ask ourselves. In this approach to learning, we have to trust that the learning is taking place or determine the learning through observation. These methods are not quantifiable; therefore, it would be difficult to enact programs like "No Child Left Behind." On the flip side, using these approaches, no child would be left behind. Each child would be recognized as gifted in some way, and those gifts would be nurtured in a very personal environment.

With this method comes less emphasis on grades and scores and more emphasis on learning at each person's own pace. It would open the door to so much fulfilled potential that we would have the delightful problem of what to do with it all. We would be faced with a way of education that would be inclusive and would allow for differences. Every day the total person would be addressed in a non-competitive, creative atmosphere. We would be challenged to rethink our educational system, considering what we value and working to order our priorities.

For five years I worked in the public elementary system in a program I designed around the theory of multiple intelligences. The idea grew out of the conclusion by the school system that our third-grade daughter, who did not take standardized tests well, was "not quite gifted enough to be in the gifted program" despite the fact that she was doing work well beyond her third-grade status. Rather than allow our daughter to continue in a classroom that was not challenging her, and reluctant to let her enthusiasm for learning dim, my husband and

I came up with the idea of one day a week operating a "flow room" centered on the intelligences. The program was launched with only two students, and soon the principal was suggesting that other "not gifted enough for the gifted program" children also take part. Soon the class grew, and I was serving twelve first through sixth graders, two with attention deficit disorder and two with bi-polar challenges, all in the same classroom, all working at their own pace, and all blossoming. The children with attention deficit were not exhibiting any of the symptoms and were attacking projects that required long attention spans. The ones grappling with the mental illness were finding a place for their ideas and learning how to operate within a group. All of the students were actively engaged.

What was happening in the classroom couldn't be measured, but it could be observed and was observed by district officials, teachers, gifted program educators, and parents. The feedback was very positive, and parents, especially, felt that their children were able to grow in many different areas. In addition, gifts that were not even imagined began to emerge. The group, working together—and this was quite a challenge for them—won Grand Prize for a film they wrote, produced, directed, and acted in at the Kan Film Festival, a film contest in the state of Kansas that spans all age groups. In addition, the group regularly presented all-school learning experiences on ancient Egypt, the rainforests of the world, and other subjects, as well as involving themselves in national and international competitions in various fields of study.

This flow room showed that children taught from the perspective of multiple intelligences can make the difference from "the gifted few" to "the many gifted."

During this time, I began to apply this theory to the religious education classroom. With new insight, I looked at God's approach to giftedness. There were students in my class who had a grasp beyond their years of what it was to be Christian. Some had a deep understanding of their spiritual person, and still others had an understanding of religious concepts that opened the door for my better understanding of them. Sadly, so many of these students were going through religious education classes and becoming bored, becoming ready to search elsewhere because we were not addressing their unique intelligences, their unique relationship with God, their unique gifts.

How do we draw out these gifts? How do we recognize them in our religious education programs? How do we help the gifted, as seen by the world, to be leaders in God's world? How do we discover the unique gifts all children have to understand their faith and their God in ways that we as teachers have not yet experienced?

Tolbert McCarroll, a religious educator and monastic, writes: "Somehow we must encourage each other to act as if the very next child we meet will become a spiritual leader who could influence the quality of life in the world to come. And we must also act as if we somehow can do something to assist that child in his or her future work. Both assumptions are probably correct. Our children desperately need us and we need them."

Our world needs gifted leaders and we have them around us—being tickled and tucked in, learning soccer and math, getting dirty and playing hard. It's time we all saw their giftedness and we all worked to make their growth in faith the very best it can be. Using the multiple intelligences theory in religious education classrooms can awaken and enhance that giftedness for the good of the whole church community and the world.

In God's world, with everyone being gifted, there is no hierarchy, and multiple intelligences make lots of sense. In God's world, there are only people with gifts, each unique, and each to be used and celebrated. The gifted people in God's world appreciate one another and look to ways in which their gifts can be shared. They look to how they can complement one another all for the glory of God.

Putting this idea into a framework of spirituality, Paul says: "There are different kinds of gifts, but the same Spirit...to each is given the manifestation of the Spirit for the common good" (1 Corinthians 12:4-7). It is surely the life work of each Christian to understand and develop the gifts he or she has been given. As parents, we must work to help our children recognize their own unique spiritual gifts. As religious educators, we must strive to awaken this understanding of giftedness in all the children to whom we minister.

There is a story told of God talking about gifts with the people in heaven:

> God pulled the chair closer. His face wrinkled in thought, his eyes shut tight. After what seemed eons, his lids fluttered open and he slowly took in the faces surrounding him. He cleared his throat.
>
> "I want to give another gift to my children on earth. They already have my Son, the greatest gift, but I want something to remind them to turn to my Son all the time, to realize they are in union with us all the time." He took in the eager faces. "What gift can I give them?"
>
> David was the first to speak. "Give them the gift of music. I've certainly used it well to remember you, to praise you." He looked at the others and nodded. "Yep, it would have to be music."
>
> Paul chuckled. "Or we could give them the gift of your sharp aim." He shook his head. "Still can't get over the fact that you got that giant with one small stone."
>
> Ruth chimed in. "But, Paul, maybe the gift should be fluency with words. Remember your words have brought so many people to God. Eloquence with words is to be cherished."
>
> Paul quickly interrupted. "But, Ruth, what about your gift with people. You are able to feel with them, nurture them, and challenge them. People feel uplifted around you. That's the real gift."
>
> This time it was God's turn to interrupt. "Hmmmmm. All of those are good but I don't know..." He lapsed into silence.
>
> John looked at God and took a leap into the conversation. "Well, God, remember when I was in the desert?

You gave me the gift of prophecy, and I was able to use that to get people's attention. Maybe that should be the gift."

"No, no, no." Simeon put down his glass. "The gift should be patience. I remember when…"

There was a big shuffle as each person present sought to stop the storyteller in his tracks.

"Just get to the point, Simeon," Paul urged.

"Patience." Simeon smiled at him. Paul slunk down in his chair. "Patience was what I needed to wait for the Savior, and that patience let me instinctively know the Savior when Mary brought him to the temple that day."

"But what about those who welcome people?" Queen Esther asked. "People like Lydia." She pointed to a slight woman at the far end of the table. "Being ready to welcome people should be the gift. It would remind us of the welcome we always receive from God."

"That's all well and good," chimed in Lydia, "but what about your real gift of thinking outside the box? You saved a whole nation doing that, and well, I might add."

Mary, who had quietly listened, now rose to speak. "I could add that acceptance should be the real gift. But I won't." She looked directly at God. "My gift of acceptance made the coming of the Savior possible, but it was John's gift and Lydia's and David's and Esther's and…all of you." She paused to look at each of them in turn. "It's everyone's gift. Those of you here and those yet to come." She turned back to God. "The gift you, my dear Creator, should give humankind is the ability to recognize their other gifts, to recognize them as part of the whole, to recognize you as the Giver, and to always be ready to help others with their special gift." She sighed. "They already have all the special gifts you gave them when you made them, but they forget. They fall into thinking one gift is better than another.

One is special, one is not. One doesn't need another." She laid her hand on God's shoulder. "With this gift, men and women would acknowledge that each one is specially gifted and all those gifts should be used for your glory."

As she sat down in her seat, God broke into the most magnificent smile, lighting up the distant corners of the universe. "Yes, the gift of acknowledging gifts. I couldn't ask for anything better."

Somewhere along the line, many of us have lost that gift from God. We fell into thinking that our gift is less or more than another's. We forgot that God intended us all to have gifts, different gifts and gifts to be used to help one another, to show one another the God in each of us. In 1 Corinthians 12:4-11, Paul tells us:

> There are different kinds of spiritual gifts, but the same Spirit gives them. There are different ways of serving, but the same Lord is served. There are different abilities to perform service, but the same God gives ability to everyone for their service. The Spirit's presence is shown in some way in each one, for the good of all. The Spirit gives one person a message of wisdom, while to another the same Spirit gives a message of knowledge. One and the same Spirit gives faith to one person, while to another person the Spirit gives the power to heal. The Spirit gives one person the power to work miracles; ...yet another, the ability to tell the difference between gifts that come from the Spirit and those that do not. To one person he gives the ability to speak in strange tongues, and to another the Spirit gives the ability to explain what is said. But it is one and the same Spirit who does all this. He gives a different gift to each person.

We, adults and children alike, need to take that special gift, that special intelligence given by God, and use it to recognize the gift of God in ourselves and in our children, to recognize the patience, the perfect aim, the music, the hospitality, the acceptance. The standard measures of good grades or intellectual ability are no more important than other gifts. We need to resurrect what God originally intended— a gifted people serving God who is Gift.

Too often we think in terms of gifts as being a small list of talents, mostly because we are taught early on that some gifts are to be cherished more than others, such as someone who is good in math or plays the piano fantastically. Or we look to IQ tests to determine the gifted around us. We need not be so narrow. God is expansive and never-ending, and we need to be likewise, especially when we look to gifts.

Let me give an example. The religious education class starts with the kids filing in from the playground. Already Johnny has shown Pete how well he can "walk the dog" with his yoyo. Kathy comes through the door, still talking, still asking questions, and very interested in what her friends have to say. David announces to the class that he has finished the latest Harry Potter book, and Jennifer waves a painting she did last evening.

The teacher settles the class and begins teaching. George gives math answers to the story of the sower and the seed. Lucy reads the Scripture beautifully, and Maria asks probing questions about the story. Devon is the first to finish the project and is eager to explain the discoveries he made. Stephanie seeks out the new girl and invites her to give her thoughts on the story. Tom compliments the teacher on the class, and Hannah daydreams as she absentmindedly waves goodbye. The class has ended, but the gifts haven't.

Too often we forget that gifts are many times quiet, performing their wonders day after day. We have to open our eyes and see the gifts around us. St. Paul explains it best when he talks of the gifts of the Spirit in Galatians 5:22-23; 6:2, 4:

> The Spirit produces love, joy, peace, patience, kindness, goodness, faithfulness, humility and self-control...Help

carry one another's burdens and in this way you will obey
the law of Christ....Each one should judge his own con-
duct for himself or herself. If it is good, then he or she
can be proud of what has been done without having to
compare it with what someone else has done."

Those gifted in intelligences not often addressed are often over-
looked and ignored by the culture of the times. We don't see the ability to
make peace or the ability to be patient or understanding as worth nurtur-
ing. We don't see the ability to listen as a gift. We assume everyone does
it, when in reality very few people have the real gift of listening.

These intelligences are very real gifts that need, almost beg, to be
shared in the world by adults and children alike. These intelligences
nurture our humanity, build our love, and strengthen our faith. They
call us to accountability in our lives. These are the multiple intelligences at work in our faith life. They call us to try new things and to develop
new thought processes, connections, and understanding beyond what
is accepted according to age. Giftedness is a "spark" of the presence of
God moving freely through all of us, enabling us to grow in phenom-
enal ways if only we open ourselves.

We are a kaleidoscope people. We come in many different shapes
and shades. We come from different backgrounds, with different family histories and different approaches to God. We carry with us a pleth-
ora of gifts, each different, each unique, each that can only be shared by
its owner. We need to unwrap those gifts in ourselves and each other so
that their beauty can fill our lives and deepen the beauty of the kaleidoscope. Working with multiple intelligences can make that happen.

We are made in the image and likeness of God—in the image and
likeness of God who is creator and gift. If children and adults hold this
to be true, we need to develop our gifts to their fullest so that, like the
Jewish tradition says, every time we walk down the street, we are pre-
ceded by hosts of angels who are saying, "Make way! Make way for the
image of God."

Not Just for Kids

Many adults grew up in a school system that measured and determined who was gifted and who was not. To embrace the approach of multiple intelligences is to open the doors to new experiences as individual intelligences are developed. For many adults, finding that there is another way to view intelligence is an experience that helps each one realize the unique gifting from their Creator.

THREE

MAKING THE RELIGIOUS EDUCATION CLASSROOM FRIENDLY TO MULTIPLE INTELLIGENCES

God said, "Let there be light," and there was light.
God saw that the light was good.
■ **GENESIS 1:3-4**

I've seen the look before. In a group of catechists who have come to a workshop on using multiple intelligences, it is quite evident. The ideas they are taking in? Great! The enrichment to their own spiritual life? Wonderful! Their belief that they can do anything like it in their classroom? Nonexistent.

Catechists faced with demands from family, friends, work, or other responsibilities often feel they are doing well if they manage the lesson plans with no major problems. They feel they have time for only the basics and see worksheets as things that can be done to reinforce the lesson without much stress. And if they adhere to the basics, they don't have to worry that something important is missed.

The beauty, though, of using multiple intelligences in the classroom is that it is supremely simple to integrate addressing the intelligences into a regular classroom plan. There are no fancy hoops to jump through, no materials to gather, no ideal to reach. Addressing multiple intelligences in the classroom actually makes the time of learning a pleasure.

There are some rules to remember if you decide to integrate multiple intelligences into your classroom and look to expanding people's vision of God and faith.

Rule No. 1: Don't try to do everything

This is important in everything we do. Too often we try to fit in every new idea, everything that needs addressing, within one sixty-minute class. It is just not possible—not possible in life's day-to-day activities and certainly not possible in a religious education classroom. Every intelligence does not have to be addressed in every class or identified in the students you work with, nor does every intelligence have to spring up in every story you tell. What is important is that you try to do *something*—something small, something large, but something. It might be playing a current popular song and then asking the children to draw comparisons between the song and the lesson of the day. Or it might be taking a work of art and seeing how the students can change it and relate it to the lesson of the day.

There are lots of possibilities if you only remember that you don't have to do everything all at once.

Rule No. 2: Take five—and possibly ten

Early in the week, take five minutes to look over the lesson for the following week. Read everything; don't assume you know what to say and do in the lesson. Once five minutes is done, let the material sit in the back of your mind. Let it occasionally surface throughout the week—the Spirit has a lot to do with this—and you will be surprised at what inspirations come your way. You might be struck with an idea that pulls all the key points together seamlessly. Or you will have an "aha!" moment that allows you to look at the material in a totally different way. Or you might be reading the paper or something online and realize how perfectly this fits into the lesson.

Taking five—and possibly ten—minutes allows for the Spirit to work in your lesson planning. When we give the material over to God, God never fails us. We do have to do our part, but the inspiration of God will come into play with the material, if we allow it.

As the ideas come to you, be sure to write them down as soon as you can. Don't trust your memory. All of us have many demands on us. Forgetting is an easy way to lose a great idea.

Rule No. 3: Don't measure

When we step into the world of multiple intelligences, we don't have a measuring system for determining whether or not material was absorbed. Gratefully, we don't need to be concerned about measuring if a child retained the information or knows the right words to the commandments. These types of measurements fall by the wayside when you work with multiple intelligences. Faith is not something that is measured. If we only want our students to know "things" about their church, then let's go with tests and worksheets. If we want faith, we can only "measure" as we talk, discuss, and embrace particular aspects of our faith.

One easy way to build talking about faith into a classroom is to have "insight time," a time where the children (and any adults too, provided they don't monopolize the conversation with what God is and isn't) are able to talk on their own levels about what they have learned about God. They will be able to share insights into their faith that worksheets are not able to give.

One time when I was subbing for a fourth-grade catechist, the lesson was centered on the miracles of Jesus, most especially the raising of Lazarus from the dead. We talked about what the word "miracle" meant and how Jesus used miracles to bring home important lessons. One girl was quiet during the discussion; finally, when we were about ready to wrap up, she raised her hand. "Do you have an insight to share, Donna?" I asked. It seemed to me that we had covered a lot of territory, and I wasn't ready for another story about how a pet was saved from harm by remembering to feed him.

"My grandma was very sick for a long time." A hush came over the class.

"She wasn't a very nice grandma. When she was well she used to yell at us to dress better or wash our hands or that we were not as good as the rest of the family." Donna swallowed. I knew whatever she was going to say was important. "When grandma got sick, my mom took care of her. You know, washing her and feeding her. Everything. Sometimes my grandma yelled at my mom, saying she didn't do things right. She said mean things, like she wished her daughter could take care of her instead. She was just being mean." Various kids in the class were shaking their head in agreement and commenting on how they would have handled that grandma. I hushed them.

"The day my grandma died, we were all in the room. It was kind of scary and kind of not. We prayed a rosary, and my dad and mom and me bent close to say goodbye to her. I was scared. But she took my hand and in a whisper said, 'I'm sorry. I love you.' And then she died."

I looked at Donna. "What do you think that says about miracles, Donna?"

"That miracles don't have to be fancy or to our liking. They don't have to be spectacular. It can be just that someone finally realizes what love is. It was a miracle that my grandma got love. It was a miracle we were all there to hear it, and it was a miracle that she died at peace. That's a miracle even bigger than Lazarus."

Donna taught the whole class that day an important truth of faith—it doesn't have to be big to mean that God is working in our lives. The miracles that come into our lives are big and little and in-between. And if we would only open our eyes, we would see that we are knee-deep in miracles every day. A powerful truth taught by a fourth grader during an insight time.

Rule No. 4: Take one risk a week

It is good to remember that sometimes the risk we take might be just to show up. Often as catechists we question our own faith because we deal with it each time we plan a lesson or teach. Sometimes it is a risk to come to the classroom and talk of God when perhaps God has been hiding from you.

Risk is part of faith. Some weeks, that risk might be letting the children share and our trusting the Spirit to enlighten us as to connections. Like the story of the rainbow fish who urged the other fish in the puddle to jump into the river and trust they would be carried to the sea, we have to trust that if we leap in, we will be carried in the arms of our God to the place we were meant to be.

Another way to take a risk is to present the material in such a way as to appeal to one particular intelligence. Perhaps the lesson is on reconciliation, and the particular intelligence you choose is musical-rhythmic. First you decide to have the class sing the blues—everything that has and is going wrong in their lives that they are responsible for. Then they write individual songs (based perhaps on songs already familiar to them) that express seeking forgiveness for a particular wrongdoing. Lastly, you have them work together on a song made up of lines by different people, each line celebrating forgiveness. End the lesson by talking about what was said in the songs and what that says about reconciliation—or sing the reflections!

Once you've taken the leap and realize that you have survived, it does become easier. However, sometimes your own personal faith life will enter into what is easy and what is difficult to do.

When my sister Barbara died, it was unexpected. She was in her early 60s and in good health and seemed to have reached a point in her life where she was going to do things she had been putting off for some time. Then one day she woke up with a cough that was violent enough to cause her rib cage to hurt. When the cough persisted for a few days, she went to the doctor, who examined her and put her into the hospital. Diagnosis? Congestive heart failure. She lived three days.

With a fifteen-year difference in age, I thought that I would not mourn her. Sure, she was my sister, but I had been away from home since I was eighteen, so it was a very casual acquaintance relationship. How wrong I was.

During a program with adults in which we were talking about integrating intrapersonal intelligence (the intelligence where a person knows herself or himself well) into a classroom setting, I used my sister Barbara as an example. As the words tumbled out, I realized that as much as I thought I knew myself, I really didn't. I was angry with God because Barbara had died. I was angry that I didn't get a chance to say goodbye.

I was fearful for my own health and well-being. In short, talking about intrapersonal intelligence forced me to confront the feelings I had about the whole painful situation, not even beginning to address the anger I felt toward God. I'm grateful that I was in a place where the people were understanding and were able to address the feelings I was having. I left that program having learned more than I believe I taught that day.

Truthful conversation about faith is never easy. It takes a lot to put our faith on the line, to trust the Spirit, to put our own egos aside. In working with multiple intelligences, you realize that there is a world of faith out there to explore and we have only touched so very little. With an ever-changing, ever-revealing God, it can be no other way. Our faith too needs to be ever-changing, ever-growing, and ever-open to the work of God and others in our lives.

Rule No. 5: Eliminate at least one worksheet a month

Worksheets bring us back to measuring. When someone answers a question or lists something on a worksheet, we have the idea that they are actually learning. Often, in reality, they are just regurgitating what is in the teacher's mind. If we want creative, thinking, sensitive members in our church, we have to encourage them to trust themselves, to allow the insights to surface and be shared.

If you eliminate at least one worksheet a month, you are demonstrating not only to the kids but to yourself that there is value in what you think and feel about God and that it is important to share that with others. A worksheet doesn't have to be replaced by anything spectacular. It can be as simple as a song, a hands-on activity, a question to cause the students to be excited about their faith. Whatever it is, it should show them that what they think and feel about God is important and needs to be shared.

Rule No. 6: Think like your students

Whenever I do creativity exercises with groups, I am amazed at the silence that ensues after I introduce the activity, especially with adults. I hold up a pencil and ask what it is and how it relates to God. After one brave soul says it is a pencil and we can write about God with it, there is total silence. If I were to do the same exercise in front of a group of kids, the answers would fly out—God is like a pencil because he writes what we need to know in our hearts...like a pencil because God is ever-new just like the pencil is ever-new sharpened...like a pencil because God points us the way we should go...like a pencil because God comes in many shapes and sizes and colors...like a pencil because there are layers to discovering God. The answers would go on and on, the creative streak in each of them coming up with ever-new, ever-changing answers.

Too many of us hang up our creative hats as we grow into adulthood. We need to put those hats on once again so we can look at what we do in a fresh light. When we begin to think like our students, we not only begin to see things differently; we are open to new insights that can be shared not only in our faith experience, but in all of our lives.

Rule No. 7: Enjoy the ride

This rule is most important. Unless we as teachers enjoy the ride, we will do nothing for our students except communicate that faith can never be fun, is always a chore, and can either be discarded as meaningless to individual lives or be dreaded because punishment is just around the corner.

If we enjoy the ride, we can laugh together, cry together, create together. We can see God as a joyful, loving God who is just waiting with surprises for us, surprises that will open our understanding of God a bit more each time.

Not Just for Kids

When you are looking to incorporate multiple intelligences into the adult faith formation classes, following these points carries much value. Too often we assume that adults enjoy writing and talking and listening to someone speak. While all these methods are well and good, it is important to address the adult's

multiple intelligences. Take a risk. Bring in music. Eliminate the
writing exercises, be creative in how you present your topic, and
above all enjoy the adults around you. Laugh, cry, and puzzle
together. That's the way faith and the intelligences grow.

Hafez, the great Sufi master, had a wonderful relationship with
God. To read his poetry is to realize how we are all called to enjoy the
ride of a wonderfully loving God.

God
Disguised
As myriad things and
Playing a game
Of Tag
Has kissed you and said,
"You're it –
I mean, you're Really IT!"
Now
It does not matter
What you believe or feel
For something wonderful,
Major-league Wonderful,
Is someday going
To
Happen.

When we take on opening our hearts and minds to using the theory of multiple intelligences in our classrooms, we open our hearts to
really being IT for God, and we can look for that major-league wonderful to happen in our classrooms and with the adults in our parishes
when we least expect it.

FOUR

INCORPORATING MULTIPLE INTELLIGENCES INTO THE LESSON PLAN

*One of our chief jobs in life, it seems to me, is to realize
how rare and valuable each one of us really is—that each
of us has something which no one else has—or ever will
have—something inside which is unique to all time.*

■ **FRED ROGERS**, EDUCATOR

E ach person has a unique way of planning a lesson. Some put
off planning until the last minute, waiting for the material
to jell in their minds before attempting to put anything on
paper or get materials together. Others meticulously plan it
throughout the week, even reading extra material on the subject to be
well prepared. Still others find a happy mix in-between. And if truth be
told, some have no lesson plan when they enter the classroom.

All these approaches are unique. Whatever your approach, there
are very real issues to take into consideration when addressing the theory of multiple intelligences in the religious education classroom.

Openness to the Spirit

First on the list of items to consider is how open you are to the Spirit of
God working in you. We've already spoken of the importance of that,
but it is an item that cannot be emphasized enough. Without openness
to the Spirit working in our classrooms, no new technique, no new ap-

proach, no new lesson plan will make a difference, because we will continue to have ourselves and our success at the center of our time with the children and will not allow God to be a part of our interaction.

Watch the details

The next item is to avoid having too detailed a lesson plan. Often teachers leave little room in their lesson planning for the teacher or the students to be creative and spontaneous. There is little opportunity for the teacher to respond to the children's immediate needs and interests. And, sadly, there are programs where the teacher receives lesson plans that have been used year after year after year. The effectiveness of these plans is never challenged, and their openness to the Spirit's work is never questioned.

Lesson plans are useful for determining what is to be covered at a particular time, but it is important to remember that these plans should never be static. We are working with living, breathing people who change and grow each and every day. What was good at one time may no longer be effective. When we look at a lesson plan as merely a tool that will enable us to remember important information that we would like to impart to our students, then we will be ready to open ourselves to changing that plan whenever and however the need arises.

Ginny was new to teaching. She took on her first-grade class with enthusiasm and dedication. When she received her teaching packet on orientation night, she was somewhat intimidated by the material that she had to read and by the directions for planning a lesson. During the orientation she was also exposed to new ideas and possibilities within her classroom. She tried to incorporate it all, but after three classes, she was in the director's office trying to tell the director that she wasn't cut out for teaching. Smart woman that the director was, she told Ginny that what was covered in orientation was to inform the teachers and offer help for them in the classroom. It was not meant to be a pattern that had to be followed each and every time. As long as the theme for the lesson is addressed, the director said, that was all that really mattered. How that was done was up to the individual teacher. Ginny was not only relieved, but she blossomed throughout the rest of the year, bringing in new ideas and approaches that the other teachers envied and wanted for their own classrooms. A great teacher who was almost lost found out that trust in the Spirit and in herself were the two most important factors in planning a lesson.

Where are the children?

When planning any lesson, you need to ask yourself some questions about the students. One of the first is "What can I expect of children at this stage of development?" When dealing with faith, this question becomes even more important, because oftentimes we assume that each child is at the same place in faith development. Adults and children alike are in a wide range of understandings of who God is and what part God plays in their lives.

Jean Piaget and later Lawrence Kohlberg addressed the different stages of moral development in children. These stages, although often occurring around the same ages in most children, are not rigid and can occur at different times in children's lives and at different instances of moral interactions. At one stage, a child might return something they stole because of the fear of being caught. At another stage, the child might return it because it is the right thing to do. These stages change and overlap depending on the situation.

According to these theories, moral thinking begins at a very primitive level when there is concern about punishment. *I do something right because I don't want to be punished.* Next is the self-interest stage, which still carries concern about punishment but also looks forward to rewards because people notice the "good" person. Next comes the good girl/good boy stage where the presence of authority urging good behavior causes someone to act out of respect and/or fear of authority. Then comes the law and order stage. More abstracting takes place, and the parent becomes the law. Personal righteousness comes from conformity to law and order. This is often where judging others takes place—the good people and the bad people. Beyond that stage comes the questioning of authority. What are the reasons for laws and rules?

This leads to the final stage, which is that of conscience and principle. This is the capability of abstracting to the universal principles upon which laws are based. At this stage people are more aware of the fact that moral dilemmas are complex and have no easy answers. People do not go through these stages in succession. Like the intelligences, they overlap. Just as someone doesn't have only one intelligence and grows to the next, these stages of moral development are not one right after the other. They ebb and flow, and decisions made in one situation might be vastly different in another.

Jane was a fourth grader who was considered the bossy one in her class. She delighted in telling other people what to do. She was quick to point out when someone did something wrong. She acted the same way in religious education class, giving the right answers and making sure that everyone knew there was a right way and a wrong way. I was quick to label her as someone who had obviously not gone beyond the law and order stage. There was a definite right and wrong in whatever Jane did.

One day in class, we were talking about the prodigal son. The whole class was having trouble with why the father took the son back and welcomed him so warmly. They all thought that he should be punished for throwing away his inheritance on gambling and for doing other bad things. They felt the older brother who stayed and did everything right was the one who should have had the fatted calf killed in celebration. Every question I raised for their consideration was shot down by someone who was in the law and order stage of development. Imagine my surprise when Jane raised her hand. I braced myself for yet another reason the prodigal son should have been punished.

"I don't think we can say he should be punished," Jane said. "He had so much going on in his head. He loved his dad, but he wanted to see what life was like outside of his village. He got along with his brother, I guess, although it doesn't say anything in the story about that." She took a deep breath. "And he certainly learned a lot of lessons during his time away from home. I think he understood his father more from being away, and, besides," she said, "it's always good when all the family is together, and that's reason to celebrate."

The conversation took a turn after that, with several of the children agreeing that he had learned some lessons. And almost all of them could relate to celebrating with families and friends. Someone whom I thought was at a dyed-in-the-wool law and order stage had smoothly and completely moved to ruling her thoughts and her heart with conscience and principle.

It is important that we catechists do not assume that the children we teach are at any particular stage, especially when it comes to who God is for them. This image of God can be at many different levels, depending on how God has been spoken of at home and at church and at school. The image of God can also change, depending on the encounters with other people as well as with God. The Spirit works in young children as well as adults. We have to be aware that some children often have a better grasp of who God is than many adults.

There is a book by Etan Boritzer entitled *What Is God?* As he explores with the children what God is, we can see that the image of God is dependent on the stage of moral development. God might be a kind old man who loves little children or an angry old man who yells at children. God might be a puzzle that goes on endlessly or the feeling we have when we love or are loved. Just as there were many images of God in this book, there are many images of God in your classroom. It is important for you as teacher to remember that, especially as you plan your lesson.

Play as life-giving

When we plan our lessons, we oftentimes leave out the factor of play. Play is a transforming, teaching influence that we need in our lesson plans. Play becomes life-giving when it awakens us to new ways of seeing ourselves as human beings and seeing God. And play applies to both children and adults. We need to plan play activities, whether they be musical chairs or a trivia game, because they draw us together as a church community. It is a delicious by-product when our play brings out insights and understanding we hadn't planned. This is evidence of the Spirit working with us. So plan those games that teach the important factors or cause the participants to work together, and watch how the Spirit works through them to touch their hearts and move them to a greater understanding of God in their life.

When working with a lesson plan and hoping to incorporate exercises that speak to the intelligences, be alert to addressing these four areas—the most important of which is being open to the Spirit. If you are following that fundamental aspect, the others will fall into place. Play will allow you to use different activities with some ease as you know the exercises will address different intelligences. And if those activities are chosen with care, the developmental and detail items will be addressed. So much happens when we are open to the Spirit, doing our part, but ready for God to step in at anytime to do God's part.

Not Just for Kids

Lesson planning doesn't stop when it gets to adults. We have to take as much care, if not more, to ensure that what we create for formation time with adults is just as fully given over to the Spirit as formation with young children. Never assume that following the same strategy year after year with adults is the way to go. Rethink your approach. Reinstill creativity into the presentation. Reinvite the Spirit to have an active part in the adult session. It is only then that we can begin to look at quality education for adults.

FIVE

PRAYER AND MULTIPLE INTELLIGENCES

By my definition, prayer is consciously hanging out with God. Being with God in a deliberate way.

■ **MALCOLM BOYD**

went to a Catholic grade school in Cleveland, Ohio. It was there that I learned how not to pray. We were told that our hands should be placed together pointing up toward heaven. We should be on our knees with our backs straight and our eyes closed. We were told to shut out all distractions, reciting the Our Father or the Hail Mary with our thoughts ever on the God who loved us—and the God who would judge us.

I failed in so many ways. My hands would creep into an intertwined position with my fingers pointing downward, and all I could think of was, "I'm pointing to hell!" The discomfort of being on my knees when I wasn't used to it caused me to sway and wiggle and get a slap on my hands from the teacher. And the Our Father? I stumbled over words I did not understand and images that only served to frighten me.

Prayer is not supposed to be that way. I so appreciated Malcolm Boyd's definition of prayer when I first heard it—"hanging out with

God." Such a beautiful concept. How many of us hang out with friends, laughing, discussing the important things of life, crying or rejoicing together over challenges, and often just being together? To think of prayer as hanging out together is to open the door to so many possibilities, so many ways of relating to our Creator.

And when you consider multiple intelligences in prayer, you open the door even wider.

The Personal Prayer Experience

As a catechist, it is important for you to examine your own background and feelings about prayer. When we examine our own prayer experience, we are able to see those areas where we are strongest in our relationship and those where we are weakest.

Here are some questions to consider:

- What is prayer like for you?
- When do you feel more in contact with God?
- When do you feel most removed?
- What awakens in you an awareness of God around you?
- What do you feel most comfortable in doing with prayer?
- Are there special prayers you cherish?
- Do you find yourself mainly praying when you need something?
- What brings you the most comfort when you pray?
- What was your best experience so far with God?

When we honestly examine what it is that we do to maintain and grow a relationship with God, we find that we approach our relationship in many different ways, based on our culture, our upbringing, and our personality. And, I would add, on our intelligences. We discover that when we talk about a relationship with God, we approach it as differently as we do a friendship with someone. We might seek the quiet in the relationship. We might seek the surprise. We might seek the formality. Whatever it is, we have to be aware of our own needs in prayer before we can attempt to fill the needs of those we are teaching.

Prayer Together

Remembering that there is no one best way to pray and that our prayer needs are as diverse as we are, the focus for prayer together should be our desire to be in worship as a community. This is what can unite us— much more so than a prescribed format for prayer.

Often in situations where we pray together, we become self-conscious. We think in terms of prayer being a very solitary activity. Too often when we pray together, we feel an urge to "get it right," to avoid long silences, to say the "right" flowery words. Prayer together, however, offers a great opportunity. We can see it as yet another opportunity to grow in relationship with our God. What becomes important is not the "rightness" of the prayer, but rather the journey we are on, the journey of falling in love with our God.

Praying together gives us the opportunity to communicate not only with God, but with each other about our relationship with God. We don't have to use only words when this communication happens. When we are together, there may be laughter, tears, or puzzlement during prayer. So much of communication happens beyond words: facial expressions, body language, tone of voice. It happens when we are full of words, as well as when we can't find the right words to say what is in our hearts.

Using multiple intelligences in prayer allows for all these different types of communication. The body can be engaged; music can help the heart beat lighter; numbers can help us order our thoughts; the visions of what can be can fill our hearts; words can flow; the sights and sounds of the world around us can give us a glimpse into divinity; light might be shed on some of the questions running throughout hearts. When the intelligences are addressed in prayer, the variety of prayer options and possibilities can only lead to a greater richness through stretching ourselves and taking that leap into the unknown—daring to grow, daring to love the God who loves us so completely.

Not Just for Kids

Praying all ways is particularly good for adults who are often stuck in the feeling that they are not doing prayer "right." Addressing the different intelligences in prayer allows for the adult person of faith to delve deeper into the mysteries of faith, oftentimes discovering a closeness and understanding that was missing in the traditional teaching of prayer. Prayer becomes more of a relationship between lovers that is woven into every hour of the day.

There are many ways to pray. It is difficult to isolate one intelligence and say that this is how you pray in this intelligence. It doesn't work that way. Just as we find it difficult to isolate only one thought—the difficulty of meditation—it is difficult to isolate the intelligences and say that this particular approach appeals only to the visual-spatial intelligence. The intelligences overlap, with one, perhaps, coming across very strongly but many of the others present.

The listing here is to demonstrate prayer that has a particular intelligence as its strongest. No one person, prayer, or activity operates solely out of a single intelligence. Instead, each has a unique combination of intelligences with one shining the strongest.

Verbal-Linguistic Intelligence

This intelligence shows a well-developed verbal skill. It has a sensitivity to the sounds, meanings, and rhythms of words, with those individuals strongest in it enjoying reading, writing, and speaking.

- *Tell a story.* Storytelling is an excellent way of prayer for this intelligence. Pick a story that you enjoy, and either read or tell it, with or without pictures or objects. Allow time for questions and comments, and then take some time to quietly reflect on what the story is saying about God, others, and faith. Regular children's books from the library are a good source, as are the parables in the Scriptures. Sometimes it is good to use a story from your own life or allow someone else to be the storyteller.

- *Utilize movies.* Praying with movies offers many possibilities. View a movie together. Take some time to reflect and then discuss. One excellent movie that opens itself for many paths of discussion is *Up.* Why was the man so reluctant to make friends with the boy? When have you missed someone the way the man missed his wife? When have you seen people responding with mean intent, like the explorer did to the man and boy? What have you wanted so much that you were willing to do anything to get it? Those are just a few question possibilities. Close with time to voice questions and give thanks to God and each other.

- *Institute a gratitude journal.* At the end of each session (or the beginning) have each person write down things for which he or she is truly grateful. At periodic times during the year bring everyone together to have a litany of gratitude, with the people using entries from their journals.

- *Use an A to Z prayer.* This prayer can take many forms. Perhaps it is a prayer of praise; then the A to Z is simply a listing of all the names or traits of God. This kind of prayer can be awesome, bubbly, creative, decisive. Allow time for reflection and end it with a resounding "Amen."

Logical-Mathematical Intelligence
This intelligence loves numerical patterns and long chains of reasoning and can discern relationships in all of it. People with this intelligence thrive on connections and consequences.

- *Use a prayer of connection.* Remember the "six degrees of Kevin Bacon"? When you played the game, you came up with connections that, within six, connected the first person to Kevin Bacon. So too the prayer of connection links us together. Pick a famous person, a person from the congregation, and a person from the classroom. Then, together, begin connecting that person until that person is connected to Jesus. For example, I like mysteries. How the world was made is a mystery. The world was made by God. God is the Father of Jesus. Jesus is connected to me. After the connections are made, take some time to reflect on the fact that we are all interconnected. We all need to take care of one another.

- *Use a timeline prayer.* Take a person from Scripture or someone from your life (or even yourself) and create a timeline of all happenings in that life. Concentrate on the faith journey, noting high and low points along that journey. Close the time with a reflection on the importance of being open to growth and change.

- *Use addition and subtraction prayers.* What are the things I see in others that I would like to add to my life? What would I like to add to make my faith life stronger? What are the things I need to subtract to achieve a stronger faith life? What things do I need to subtract to draw me closer to God? This prayer can take on many characteristics of addition and subtraction in our lives—prayer life, family life, how I treat my friends, and what I do with my free time.

- *Use a mathematical problem prayer.* Take any mathematical problem appropriate for the age group you are with. For example, the conference planned for seven attendees. The kitchen has ten apples for the attendees. Twenty-five people showed up. How can the apples be shared so everyone gets some? Give the participants the problem, and challenge them to come up with identifying the life problem and how it can be solved. Caution that you are not looking for a mathematical answer to the problem, but rather an answer to what situation in life is similar to this problem. After members of the group have figured out the situation, allow them to—either individually or together—get "answers" for the life problems. End again with time for reflection.

Musical-Rhythmic Intelligence

Musical-rhythmic intelligence is the ability to produce and appreciate rhythm, pitch, and timbre and to appreciate various forms of musical expression. This intelligence is also sensitive to the sounds of the environment and the human voice. Using musical rhythmic intelligence when we pray allows us to get in touch with the natural rhythm of life, the rhythm of God. It is musical rhythm that will follow us throughout our mortal lives and into eternal life.

- *Pray through advertisements.* Watch one or two advertisements on television. Take the challenge to turn that commercial into a prayer about God. What words would change, if any? What images, if any? What rhythm of the song would be different or what does the present rhythm say about God? Watch the commercial again together and end with shared reflections about what was learned about God.

- *Sing the blues.* Talk together about some of the struggles individuals are going through, struggles the world is facing. Discuss together how that makes a person feel. Zero in on one universal feeling—and if that isn't possible, choose a few—and together write a song of the blues about that difficult time. When the composition is finished, join together and pray your blues song.

- *Develop a musical timeline.* Have participants make timelines of the important faith moments in their lives or times when they especially felt the presence of God. Have them think of a song or instrumental music or created rhythm that conveys in part the feeling of those special moments. For example, the loss of a grandmother might elicit a sad rhythm; the birth of a brother, a happy song. When it comes to sharing, ask each person to choose one moment and its corresponding song or melody to offer as the prayer.

- Make a *Musical Prayer Creation.* Get a paper and pencil, or, if preferred, paper and paints for each participant. Choose a song. Have everyone sit down with paper and pencil or paints in hand, close their eyes, and listen to the music. Participants begin to draw or paint as the music touches them. Urge them to concentrate on God guiding their hands and hearts. Tell them that, when they feel ready, they should draw or write what is coming to mind. When the music ends, invite the participants to share what insights surfaced.

Visual-Spatial Intelligence
Visual-spatial intelligence is the capacity to think in images and pictures, to visualize accurately and abstractly. It is the ability to see beyond the reality in front of us to create new ways of relating to and appreciating the world. Visual-spatial intelligence is manifest in people like the apostle Thomas. They find it easier to make a leap of faith when they are able to make a connection between the picture in their minds and the concrete. People with this strong intelligence are our navigators, sculptors, architects, painters, and graphic design artists. This is the intelligence that adds dimension to our lives and, when invited, can add dimension to our faith, taking us places we never imagined we could go.

- *Use guided meditations.* Because this intelligence is so good at imagining, the guided meditation is of much value. Guided imagery meditations are available in numerous books, or they can be written to meet a particular need. For a guided meditation, have class members find a comfortable spot, take a deep breath, and close their eyes. Let them become calm with several deep breaths, and then begin taking them on the journey the meditation offers. Perhaps the meditation is on water and its life-giving qualities, or it is a time with Jesus as he works miracles. Whatever it is, let the journey become individual. Include time for the participants to talk with God silently about what they are thinking and feeling.

- Pray a *scarf prayer.* Give each person a scarf. Become centered. Concentrate on everything God has given, knotting or untying the scarf as the different ideas, objects, and thoughts come into play, thereby allowing the scarf to change. When the prayer draws to a close, put the scarf on and let the blessings cover you.

- *Make the Sign of the Cross.* We often sign ourselves without any thought to what we are actually doing. Take time to pay attention to how the Sign of the Cross is made. Consider the words: "In the name of the Father...and of the Son...and of the Holy Spirit...Amen." Essentially this simple prayer says that all we say and do is done for God.

- *Pray for another.* Start with a squiggle shape into which you put the name of the person you want to pray for. Add detail such as dots, circles, or lines to the drawing. Add color to the drawing and extra squiggle shapes to denote other people if this person reminds you of others. Continue to enhance the drawing until it feels finished. When it is completed, contemplate the drawing and remember this person in a very special way.

Bodily-Kinesthetic Intelligence

The body is a great gift, one that we too often ignore. Howard Gardner defines bodily-kinesthetic intelligence as the ability to use the body to express emotion, as in dance, body language, and sports. He says that it is the ability to learn by doing. It is the intelligence of the whole body. You can't be bodily-kinesthetic and not move. Take time to consider how wonderfully your body is made, and begin now to use it as a very important part of your prayer for yourself and those you teach.

- *Pray against abandonment.* Sit down, wrap your arms around yourself, and hold yourself. Do this in whatever way is comfortable for you. Create a warmth around you, an enclosed hug-like feeling. Imagine God holding you, telling you God will always be with you and will never abandon you.

- *Use Play-Doh® prayers.* Julia McGuinness, in her book *Creative Praying in Groups* from Liturgy Training Publications, has several great ideas for using this child's clay in prayer session. One of them is what follows: Give each student a ball of Play-Doh®. Have them shape it into a ball and then imagine it as being the earth. Think about being a tiny speck on this planet. Think of all the other people. Pause to remember them in prayer. Now see that same ball as a large stone, the stone that was in front of Jesus' tomb. Reflect on Jesus being alive and how we need to be Jesus to one another. Roll the Play-Doh® into a long, thin spaghetti shape. Your hands are probably now somewhat grainy from the Play-Doh®. Reflect on how God gets into our lives and gets messy for us. Note now the loose ends of this spaghetti roll and reflect how those ends represent the people on the rim of our society. Now form a ring and reflect on how we need to bring all people into our circle. Finally, make a small bowl. Reflect on how God forms us, molding us to be the best people we can become. Hold the bowl in your hands and become aware of God holding you, warming you, and loving you.

- *Walk the labyrinth.* Labyrinths were used a great deal in medieval times to have participants center on God, working through problems or stresses as they walked the path, which consists of one way in and one way out. Today, there are some places with labyrinths, but you don't have to go far to "walk" a labyrinth. One of the easiest ways is to take a piece of paper and draw a continuous line from one point to an end point. Now, take one finger and slowly trace that line from beginning to end. Gradually increase the difficulty of the line until all your concentration is focused on getting from one point to the other. Such an activity frees our minds to listen to God's thoughts on the challenge we are struggling with.

- *Dance your prayer.* Lots of possibilities exist for this. It is a wonderful means of prayer. If you are too self-conscious about dancing, try clapping, jumping, swaying, turning, bending, or pointing. Anything that involves the body is a way to give praise and to connect with God through bodily-kinesthetic intelligence. Consider choreographing a well-known passage from Scripture and performing it for God. Get as elaborate or as simple as you wish.

Naturalist Intelligence

Naturalist intelligence is sensitivity to the natural world. It is a keen ability to recognize and categorize plants, animals, and other objects in nature and to realize how all these elements interact with each other. This intelligence invites us to stand still and take in the world around us and to reflect on our role in the world. People with a strong naturalist intelligence are in love with nature. Given the right opportunities, nature can help them fall deeply in love with the Creator.

- *Five minutes there, five minutes back.* In this prayer the group walks for five minutes, being sensitive to their surroundings and recording their findings. Then they return during the next five minutes. Upon their return they discuss what they saw and heard and smelled and end with a prayer of thanks for the special awareness that comes from special walks.

- *A study of one.* Choose something, such as a leaf, a flower, or a shell from the natural world. Close your eyes and touch it. Keep your eyes closed as you become familiar with it. Learn everything you can about this object through your senses before considering what God might be saying about it and what significance might be attached to it. Ask God to show you what you can learn from this object of the world, this object of nature. Appreciate God's creation and give thanks.

- *The Maker, Keeper, and Lover.* Julian of Norwich had a reflection with a hazelnut. As she held it in her hands, she realized that the whole world was in that hazelnut, and it did not suddenly disappear. She realized it was because God was the Maker, the Keeper, and the Lover. From time to time in your classroom, bring in something from nature. Have the children contemplate that God is the Maker, Keeper, and Lover of this object, and invite them to bask in the gift of God as our Maker, Keeper, and Lover.

- *Hearing nature.* There are many recordings around of different sounds of nature—waves hitting the shore, the sounds of the forest, and the wind through trees. Pick one of these recordings and have the students close their eyes and just listen, paying attention to the scene it evokes. Ask them to feel themselves at the place that has come to mind. Have them imagine hearing God's voice calling them to be part of creation, to be good stewards.

Interpersonal Intelligence

This intelligence has the strong ability to detect and respond appropriately to the moods, motivations, and desires of others. This intelligence enables people to be in harmony with one another and to have the ability to work cooperatively in a group, as well as the ability to communicate both verbally and non-verbally with others. When we nurture our prayer life by using our interpersonal intelligence, we nurture not only ourselves but the total community as we grow ever more aware of the connection between God and each of us.

- *Blessing cup.* Have a special cup in your classroom used for the blessing cup ritual. These rituals can be made by the students, or you could use the book *The Blessing Cup* by Rock Travnikar, OFM. The rituals revolve around various occasions—birthdays, new member, baptism—and each of those occasions are shared with the blessing cup and with the ritual around it. The emphasis is our connection to each other and to our God.

- *Where will you be tomorrow?* This simple prayer opportunity connects us to one another. Go around the room and ask everyone where they will be at a specific time the next day. Ask also if there is anything that is happening that they would like the group to pray for. Then challenge the class to remember at the specific time the next day to pray for each other, remembering the needs and challenges being faced by each and every one of them. This is an excellent prayer to emphasize connectedness.

- *Parable prayer.* As a group, write a parable together, each person writing a different portion of the story. Tell the parable together, discuss what it has to say about faith, and take some time to reflect on what we have taught one another through the parable.

- *Newspaper stories.* From a newspaper or the Internet, choose a story about someone who has gotten into some type of trouble. Together read the story and talk about it. Discuss whether or not you can pray for this person and what type of help the person might need. Take some time to imagine how you would feel and what you would think if you were this person. Pray together for that person and for more compassion for those who suffer.

Intrapersonal Intelligence

This intelligence is the intelligence of the people who know themselves well. They know their feelings and emotional responses and are often given to self-reflection. They have a great sense of the spiritual and look at the deeper picture not readily seen. As your class grows in prayer, especially using the intrapersonal intelligence, you will find that the knowledge and insights gained from God surface again and again to guide your students' behavior and decisions—and your own as well.

- *Prayer mat.* Within your classroom have a special blanket or rug. This will become the class's prayer mat. You might consider dedicating it to prayer at the beginning of the year. The mat is available to use every class by anyone who needs some time to talk with God alone. The mat is spread out, and the person simply sits, lies, or kneels and becomes quiet and begins to listen. Those using the mat are asked just to become aware of God around them and to listen, acknowledging what God has been doing for them and placing before God any needs. Above all, they are urged to simply be quiet and rest in God.

- *Scripture person prayer.* Choose a person from Scripture. Reflect on that person and imagine the challenges they might have encountered. Take some time to pray as that person might have prayed, and close your time praying as only you can.

- *Mindfulness.* Teach your students the importance of being alert to the moments of grace, to the chances to be grateful, to the signs of the Spirit. Talk to them about paying attention, about being mindful of the things and people we overlook or take for granted. Encourage them to practice mindfulness. Introduce them to little things that can help them be mindful, such as the ring of a phone calling them to attention or a beautiful flower reminding them about God.

- *Ethical will.* Give an opportunity for your children to write an ethical will, a will that leaves to people what one believes and holds dear. Perhaps make this into a few sessions. In the first session, the children consider the values they hold and whom they would like to gift; in the second session, the children write their wills; and in the final session, invite the children into a prayerful sharing of what individuals felt during the exercise and perhaps some of the elements of their wills. This prayer keeps us in touch with gifting the world with our persons.

Existential Intelligence

This intelligence asks the hard questions—Who am I? Why am I here? What am I to do with my life? When will I know if something is right for me? How will I be in a particular situation? With this intelligence, there is a sensitivity and capacity to tackle profound questions about human existence. People with a strong existential intelligence think beyond the box, beyond the pain, beyond the joy. They think about eternity. Existential intelligence has us considering God's plan for our lives and how that will impact not only those around us now but also those yet to come. When we pray existentially, we connect to all the hard questions of life, maybe never getting an answer, but joyfully searching.

- *The question.* Give each person a piece of paper. Present one question, such as "What is heaven like?" Allow them time to think and write about it. Share what is written on the papers, and then discuss how everyone's idea of heaven is different. Sit quietly as a group and listen to what God has to say about the question.

- *On the floor.* Participants lie on their backs, not touching one another, and close their eyes. Help them, if necessary, to relax their bodies, becoming quiet within themselves. Now ask one question, such as "Why do people suffer?" Let the individuals become quiet, only asking them to be quiet and listen for what God has to say on the question. After a time, ask them to open their eyes and perhaps write what they heard.

- *The pet connection.* In quiet time, have the students consider how pets teach us important truths about life. Have them consider what they learn from pets. How are we called to be good caregivers for them? Talk about all the various ideas, and then take some time to listen to what God has to say.

- *Why did God make you?* Everyone is given a sheet of paper. Have each person number from one to five, and next to each number list a reason why God made us. Once that is done, ask the participants to write down how the reasons God made them as individuals might change the way they live their lives. Share and reflect.

Not Just for Kids

Praying with the intelligences is an opportunity for adults to open up more fully to God, too. Too often, adults use only one approach to prayer, and that approach often leads them to not praying or worrying if they are doing it "right." By using different approaches to address different intelligences, the entire person is called into the prayer. We are better able to see that God is working in all aspects of our lives. Introducing this approach in faith formation programs for adults broadens what is possible in prayer encounters.

Pope John XXIII said, "Prayer is the raising of the mind to God. We must always remember this. The actual words matter less." Based on those words, I think John XXIII heeded Malcolm Boyd's words and did a lot of hanging out with God, the way those who pray with their intelligences do. The actual words don't matter. The journey does.

SIX

MULTIPLE INTELLIGENCES
AND THE SACRAMENTS

I have looked into your eyes with my eyes.
I have put my heart near your heart.

■ **POPE JOHN XXIII**

One year, I had ten preschoolers in my class. One of the stations in the classroom was the ongoing preparing of wheat into flour. Each class, at least one student, possibly more, took an opportunity to make some flour. It was no easy task. Using a mortar and pestle, they had to take a small amount of wheat and crush it into the tiniest possible particles. It took a great deal of pounding, many tears (when the wheat spilled), and an occasional yelp of pain as the pestle nipped a little finger instead of the wheat. In early April, we finally had enough "flour" to attempt making bread. Together we mixed the flour and water and salt and kneaded and kneaded and kneaded it until it was smooth and elastic. The big moment came when we put it in the oven and waited for it to bake. The delicious aroma of baking bread floated through all the classrooms.

Finally it was done and ready for eating. We blessed the bread, broke it, and shared it with one another. It was unanimous that it was the best-tasting bread ever. When class was over, a fifth grader came in to pick up his brother. He asked to have a piece of bread. He tasted it, spit it out, and said how horrible it was. His younger brother, Bryan, looked at him and said, "You didn't taste the laughs and the hurts."

Upon reflection I realized that Bryan had a great deal of wisdom at his young age. The bread wasn't really any type of bread to write home about. What it was was a culmination of eight months of working on that flour. That bread did indeed have all the hurt fingers, the spilled flour, and the happiness of reaching four cups.

That's the essence of sacrament. Each sacrament is a sign of God's grace, but it is also a sign of our willingness to grow, to work, to share joy and pain, and to celebrate together. Ask any of the students I have had over the years about the sacraments, and they will often give the definition and complete it with the line "and we celebrate together as community the love we share with each other and with God."

Addressing multiple intelligences in the teaching of the sacraments allows us to emphasize that community aspect, that interconnectedness, with joy and sorrow and celebration. Sacraments do not happen just in the church; they begin in what has already been happening in people. Sacraments are lived long before they are celebrated. For example, many people have a sense of the presence of God in them and in the community. When they celebrate Eucharist, they realize that this is indeed something to be celebrated in a special way.

The word "sacrament" in the widest sense is any person, place, thing, or event where we encounter God in a new and different way. This might be an "aha!" moment during a concert, or a moment of reflection during a sunset, or "come and see" uttered by a small child. This encounter—and that could be any such encounter—somehow changes us and our understanding and acceptance of God.

The sacraments as we know them in church have their roots in this broader definition. All the sacraments come from human experience. All of them mark moments of importance in a person's life. And all of them are meant to be celebrated.

I was having dinner at a friend's house. I had happened to have had her son in religious education for two different years. Somehow or other, we had gotten into telling stories of things that happened in class, and remembering helped us laugh and get a bit sad and talk about how hard some things were to do. Jon then piped up and said, "That's one thing we learned. Every sacrament was worth celebrating." The "definitions" of the sacraments went something like this that night: baptism involves babies and dunking and celebrating. Eucharist means lots of work grinding and baking and celebrating. Reconciliation is playing Jeopardy so we remember the important points about the sacrament, along with hugs and celebration. Confirmation is saying yes and celebrating, and marriage is committing and celebrating. Holy orders is vowing and celebrating, and the sacrament of the sick is mourning and crying and remembering and celebrating. The definitions could have been crisper but the essence was there—celebration.

Probing a little deeper with Jon showed that he considered sacraments as opportunities to grow closer to God and to the community and to celebrate that togetherness. He added that, yes, there are seven sacraments but most importantly there is the eighth sacrament, and that is manifest in the people we meet each and every day.

You might say, using those definitions, that the sacraments address the intelligences through symbols, words, body language, concept, and meaning. The sacraments are perhaps the few "all in one" approaches to the intelligences. Let's see how that is possible.

Baptism

Baptism is a celebration of belonging to the community and to God. It is a step of initiation signaling the beginning of a relationship that continues to grow as we grow in recognizing our privileges and responsibilities. It is a sacrament full of symbolism and thus ideal for a journey in multiple intelligences.

All of the following activities are but jumping-off points for further discussion on the sacrament and conversation on the encounters with God in baptism.

- *Create a "baptism newspaper."* Items to include might be:

   Shields of baptism signaling adoption through baptism

Flag for the country of God where baptized persons are citizens

Original crossword puzzle on baptism

Written haiku or other poetry on baptism

Advertisement on baptism as space fillers

Article on celebrating baptism in the home

Article "written by a little old lady who looks back on her life and says, 'It all began with baptism.'"

An original responsive prayer on baptism

- *Prepare baptismal bumper stickers.* Specify that only seven letters or numbers are to be used and that you want to convey a good message about baptism. This is an excellent activity for the visual-spatial intelligence.

- *Baptismal anniversary cards.* Have each person write his or her name, baptism date, and full address on a slip of paper. Put these in a box and draw names. Each person is to make a baptismal anniversary card for the person whose name they draw. Provide envelopes that can be addressed immediately, with the baptismal date in the upper right corners of the envelope.

- *Names.* Do an exploration of each person's name—what country did it come from, what is the meaning, how does it talk about the individual's uniqueness?

- *Remembering.* Take some time for the students to recall how their baptism was celebrated. Let them put together a celebration of their baptism as they would have liked to have had it celebrated.

- *Decorate.* Decorate the classroom as it might be for a baptismal celebration. Encourage all the students to take an active part in the celebrating. Use plenty of symbols, and try to create an atmosphere that demonstrates to people as soon they walk in that they are going to celebrate baptism.

- *Prayer.* Working as a group and using the symbols of the sacrament of baptism, create a prayer time that will bring baptism alive for everyone. Perhaps it is a receiving line ready to welcome the newly baptized. Or maybe it is a dance that will be taught to all of the participants. The celebration can encompass any or all aspects. This is a difficult job when you take into account the ages and backgrounds of the people who will be attending the celebration. Make it as inclusive as possible. This might take a few classes and much discussion, but the celebration at the end will be well worth it to everyone in the classroom and in attendance.

It is up to you as the catechist to make the connections from the activities to the sacrament. Don't, however, feel that it is entirely up to you. Open the way for the Spirit to inspire, to direct, to touch the hearts of those in attendance to also have comments that will help the community grow. You don't have to do it all yourself. After all, through baptism you have a whole family of people just waiting for the opportunity to talk about God.

Reconciliation

Perhaps the best and simplest definition of reconciliation is that the sacrament is a reminder that God loves us, no matter what. It gives us a concrete sign of God helping us to reconcile with God, ourselves, and each other, and it gives us an opportunity to celebrate forgiveness.

Some of the suggested ways to learn about reconciliation and to celebrate forgiveness might be in the following activities that address the various intelligences.

- *Take a course in light.* Have students consider times when they have felt like a particular kind of light. Perhaps it is a bug light or a floodlight or a neon light or a fluorescent light or a pen light. Let them discuss why they felt like a particular light when they did. Draw a connection to talking about reconciliation being a chance to bring light back into our lives because sin causes our light to dim and even go out completely.

- *Broken and restored.* Each person receives an envelope with pieces of a heart. The five pieces are numbered, and the students are asked to write or draw on each numbered piece:

  One time you broke something on
  your body or hurt something

  Something that you own that is broken right now

  A time you fixed something for someone

  One thing you'd like to fix about yourself

  A time when Jesus helped you "shine"
  again after you were broken

Talk about how sin damages us and reconciliation restores us. As you speak, have the students begin putting their hearts together bit by bit. Take time to talk about the various aspects of reconciliation and how sorrow and forgiveness are the important parts of reconciling with God and with others and with ourselves.

• *City without time to forgive.* There is an excellent story that brings out the importance of forgiveness. It is most effective if it is acted out with all the students participating.

> The story goes that there was a town that a person came to, and he was greeted at the hotel by a man who gave him a ticket to wear around his neck. He was told that if he valued his life he should stay in his room until he left in the morning. The man thought that an odd command and decided he wouldn't give it a second thought.
>
> On his way to the elevator, he accidentally stepped on a man's shoe. The man scowled at him, pulled out a hole punch, and punched the person's ticket, scowling that "you stepped on my shoe!"
>
> When he got to his room he found the maid finishing up, and he accidentally bumped her while unpacking his suitcase. She gave him a punch on his ticket. When he went down to the restaurant to eat, an old man looked at him and sadly shook his head. "You want to leave town in the morning? You had better stay in your room."
>
> The person asked him what he meant. The old man replied, "Here in this town we don't have time to forgive, so we just keep track of what people do to one another to hurt them. Those are the punches. You get six punches and you are no longer part of the town. We kill you because you are doing too many things wrong. Poor Mrs. Iverson is holed up in her house and refuses to leave. She has five punches, and she wants to live. Heck of a way she's living now if you ask me."
>
> The person couldn't believe what the old man was saying. "You mean people can't forgive here?"

After the story is told or acted out, discuss:

What would it be like to live in a community without forgiveness?

How long could any of us live without God's forgiveness?

What makes us different because of God's forgiveness?

You might also act out the play so that people replace the holes punched from the tickets. What type of transformation takes place? This is excellent for all intelligences especially if the decision is made to act the story out.

• *Forgiveness looks, sounds, feels like this.* During this activity, which appeals to many of the intelligences, students get an opportunity to really consider forgiveness.

Express, through the use of finger paints, feelings you have in the crunch of sin, in the confession of sin, and in the joy of being forgiven. Remember to take into account color choice.

Lyric writing will allow for the expression of forgiveness through song. You could suggest they take a song with which students are familiar and change the lyrics to mirror what forgiveness looks, sounds, and feels like.

A scavenger sculpture made of found or recycled materials will allow for the use of all sorts of materials to create a sculpture that speaks about an aspect of reconciliation—sin, sorrow, confession, forgiveness, celebration. Use as many different materials as possible.

Read a few parables together and discuss the characteristics of a parable. Have individual students or groups write a parable of forgiveness.

From a pile of different magazines, choose various pictures that speak about forgiveness. Have individuals or groups put them together in a collage of forgiveness.

- **Fruit basket.** This game opens itself to many possibilities even beyond use with reconciliation. For this particular sacrament the "fruits" would be "sin," "sorrow," "penance," "reconciliation," and "celebration."

  Everyone is seated in a circle in chairs, except for the person in the middle. That person chooses one word or two and when those words are called out, the people with those words (whispered to them before the game begins) have to get up and find another chair. Whenever the word "celebration" is said, everyone gets up and finds a different chair. This is not only a type of community work, but also a good way for the students to remember the key elements of the sacrament.

- **Types of sin.** Each group of students is given a particular type of sin. Groups are asked to discuss the kind of sin that they have, make a list of concrete examples of that particular kind of sin, and talk together about the consequences of such a sin in a person's life. Finally, the group is to prepare some type of presentation to the other groups about the type of sin that their group has, allowing for the large group to guess the type of sin that is being presented.

  Acts of commission. You are involved in doing something wrong or failing to do something God expects you to do. You know the act is wrong but for some reason you are doing it anyway.

  Acts of omission. For example, you know that there is a housebound neighbor on your street who wants you to run simple errands for him, like dropping off his books at the library or picking up a few things at the store. You decide you don't like the neighbor enough to give him your time. You even walk around the block to avoid passing his house.

When dealing with reconciliation and attempting to address the intelligences, be sure to always bring your activities full circle. Don't talk about sin without sorrow, sorrow without forgiveness, or forgiveness without celebration. Also make use of the ritual of the sacrament. Talk about the laying on of hands. Discuss what it is like to do penance. Talk about healing and how it can affect many areas of our lives. Call everyone to imagine a life where reconciliation is rampant, where people seek forgiveness and acknowledge their wrongdoings and rejoice together in the loving God we call Father.

Eucharist

This sacrament is central to the life of the community. In this sacrament we offer adoration, praise, gratitude, sentiments of repentance, and heartfelt petition. It is a meal that sustains us in spirit and helps us to reach out and share Jesus with others in the community. The sacrament is a celebration of unity and love. Addressing the multiple intelligences when teaching this sacrament allows the students to see the all-encompassing call to love God and one another.

- *Dinnertime.* Prepare a dinnertime meal or snack meal together. Set a table. Have fancy dishes and silverware. Place the food in the center of the table. Say a prayer of blessing. Eat. Clean up, washing the dishes and putting any remaining food away. Gather to talk about what happened. Make comparisons to what takes place in the Mass. Talk about how a meal brings us together. What do you think Jesus had in mind with the institution of the Eucharist?

• *Bread baking.* Many suggestions are out there about in-corporating bread making into the classroom. Perhaps the easiest might be to make matzo bread. You can tell the students about how this was very similar to the bread made by the Israelites as they fled Egypt. Simple recipe: 4 cups of flour. Work one stick of butter into the flour as if making a piecrust. Add one cup of water to begin with and begin stir-ring and kneading. Add more water as needed. Keep knead-ing. Everyone can take a turn. Kneading should take about 20 minutes. Let it rest for about 5 minutes and then break into four balls. Roll out each ball and cut shapes—perhaps a circle with an appropriate symbol in it. Bake at 400 degrees for about 20 minutes. It helps if you place another (bottom greased) cookie sheet on top to prevent curling. Break bread together in an appropriate ceremony when it is finished.

• *Have each person bring in something connected to someone who has died in their family or no longer lives close enough to them to see each day.* Put all the offerings together on the prayer table and talk together about each one. What memo-ries does the item evoke? What other memories do you have of this person? What do you do to remember them? Draw comparisons between their special someone and Jesus and the Eucharist.

• *For the logical-mathematical intelligences in your class, pose the problem of how many people have received Eucha-rist over the years.* Start with twelve apostles and go from there. See what comes up and what discussion ensues. Keep it open-ended and be sure to point out the portion from the Mass that talks about "from age to age you gather a people to yourself."

Eucharist is a celebration of our unity with each other and with the risen Christ. When we use activities that address the multiple intelligences, we are opening the door to greater growth in understanding this great mystery of our religion.

Confirmation

This sacrament has been under discussion for what seems like forever. Originally confirmation was received at the same time as baptism. Its intent was to complete baptismal grace and enrich the receiver with special strength from the Holy Spirit so as to be able to spread and defend the faith. This, of course, meant a commitment to a life of developing faith. Further down the road, the celebration of baptism and confirmation was separated, and then the age dispute began. Adults, teenagers, young children? The essence of the sacrament, however, remained the same.

- *Forced-choice activity.* Prepare ten statements and set up four "centers" with "agree," "sort of agree," "sort of disagree," and "disagree." Some of the statements might be: "I feel teenagers should have the right to choose what they want to wear to school" or "I enjoy going to church on Sunday." Make sure your ten statements come from various areas of values. When a statement is read, ask the students to move to the area that identifies that item for them and then to discuss with the others around them why that response was chosen. After a bit, go on to the next question, using as much time as necessary. This exercise allows the students to make choices and to explore why they or others make the same or different choices. Because confirmation is about deepening our commitment to a particular path to God, it is important that values are discussed.

- *The Sermon on the Mount.* Break the class into groups. Ask each group to read the Sermon on the Mount. When the groups are done, give each of them a particular part of the sermon. Discussion takes place around that part, along with a presentation of what Jesus asks of us in light of that Scripture section. Presentations can range from music to skits to math problems to drawings to whatever blossoms from the discussion.

• *Symbols of confirmation.* The two major symbols of confirmation are oil and touch. Have before the students a sample of the oil. Talk about how this is a special oil and a sign of our unity and that it is perfumed as a reminder of how our virtue should sweeten everyone's lives. Talk about how athletes used to be rubbed with oil before big events. Then discuss the laying on of hands as a gesture of blessing and healing and also as a symbol of belonging. After the discussion and exploration are through, anoint and lay hands on each other in a prayerful end to your time together.

Confirmation is the commitment to a Christian lifestyle. It calls us to care for one another and to be a support to each other as we follow Christ. If we are open to one another, we will learn that we can develop with each other, sharing our intelligences and being always open to growth.

Marriage

Marriage is the sacrament of commitment between two people who love each other. Before God, they pledge their love and commitment to growth together. The couple is open to children as an expression of their love and are ever willing to have their love impact the greater community.

• *Married how long?* Using a tally sheet, figure the number of years of marriage in the families represented in your classroom. Include every year of married life that exists in the room, including grandmothers and grandfathers, aunts and uncles, if the children know how long they have been married. Talk about what might have happened during those

many years of marriage. What was difficult? What was easy?
How did these marriages deal with the coming of children?
If the class doesn't know the answers to these questions, have
them imagine.

• *Hard times.* Break into small groups. Give each group a situation that can happen in a marriage, and have them consider
what was difficult and what might have been easy within
that situation. Let them determine if what happened is
enough to end a marriage. Talk about how it is not always
easy to love and the very real fact that some couples have
difficulties so great they cannot overcome them. They might
not be able to live together in love, and they may decide it is
better not to live together any longer. Discuss how this hard
decision might impact the other members of the family. It
is important to discuss this aspect when talking about marriage because divorce and separation are becoming more and
more the reality in our lives. We need to know and remember that sometimes things do not work out, but separation
does not make God love them any less.

• *Plan a wedding.* Create two mythical people who are going
to get married. Together plan a wedding. Accept any ideas—
about the type of dress, the number in the wedding party,
the dinner itself, any special things that are to be done. Write
the vows and petitions, and plan the ceremony itself. After
all the planning is done, have a group figure out the ballpark
cost of carrying off such a celebration. Together discuss how
this wedding ceremony will be helpful to the marriage. How
will the wedding ceremony hurt the marriage? What is more
important—the wedding or the marriage? Why?

• *Wedding song.* People pick out different songs for their weddings. Once the class has discussed marriage and weddings,

have them compose a wedding song that has within its verses what people should celebrate in a wedding and what is most important in a marriage.

By bringing an opportunity for discussion about marriage to your students and supplying them with activities that will nudge their intelligences, you give them more of an opportunity for a successful marriage.

Holy Orders

This is a sacrament of special service to the community. Bishops, priests, and deacons are ordained to preach and teach, to celebrate the sacraments, and to build the community. While bishops, priests, and deacons share in Christ's priesthood in a special way, all of us who are baptized share in Christ's priesthood. We are called to hear and share God's word. We are called to celebrate the Eucharist and the other sacraments. Most of all, we are called to share our unique talents with the church. We are called to share our intelligences so as to help others grow in their intelligences.

- *Gift flags.* Each person in the room designs a flag that showcases the gift or ministry that they can share with the community. Use whatever materials are available. Keep them and "fly" them each time you gather for prayer.

- *Homily time.* Each student prepares a five-minute homily to be presented to the class. This homily can center on the gift they have to share with the community or on the service aspect of holy orders. This will entail some research, as they are asked to include one Scripture reference.

- *Vestments.* Research together the symbolism of the vestments worn at Mass. Where did they originate? What is the meaning for today? Discuss thoughts on whether or not these vestments should continue to be part of the eucharistic celebration.

- *What makes a good leader?* People who receive holy orders are called to be leaders. Brainstorm together what makes a good leader and especially what makes a good leader in the church. Also consider this question: "If there is a leader in our church, do we follow that leader without thinking or questioning? Why or why not?"

Holy orders is a sacrament of service, and by using the intelligences to examine the sacrament, we come away with a deeper understanding of our call to the priesthood and the call to service.

Sacrament of the Sick

One of the best-kept secrets of the church is the sacrament of the sick. This sacrament is so precious and so effective and so available, but it is requested so infrequently. This lack of use is a sign of our lack of understanding of this sacrament.

Suffering and death have always plagued us. This sacrament gives us an opportunity to celebrate the healing ministry of Jesus and calls us to remember the importance of our ministry to the sick and dying of our community.

- *People I know.* Make a list of all the people you know. Think about them, and consider whether they are in need of Jesus' healing touch. Discuss together what makes the need for the touch important. Tell stories about the times that Jesus used a healing touch.

- *Hands as symbols.* Take some time to examine each other's hands. Note the crevices and the nails and anything that is interesting. Look at your own hands. Talk about the different ways in which we use our hands. Extend that conversation to how we use those hands to comfort one another. Take some time to demonstrate the healing touches that we give to one another—handshake, hand on the shoulder, hug, touching a cheek, etc. Take it a step further by going through the different hand gestures that are used in church rituals. Close the time by laying hands on each other.

- *The ritual of the anointing of the sick.* Go through the ritual from beginning to end, explaining things as the ritual moves along. Actually running through the ritual will help the children in particular see that it is not something to be afraid of, but rather that it is a comforting ritual for those who are in need of healing.

- *Doctor, doctor.* Determine at the start of the session that the classroom is a hospital room. Two people are given special assignments: one as a doctor and one as a priest. Everyone else is assigned an illness. Each person acts out and talks about their illness and decides whether to call a doctor, priest, or both. At the end of the session, talk about who, based on what took place, should receive the sacrament and why. Encourage the children to talk about all the reasons given or not given and whether or not Jesus' healing touch was needed.

Most people who have received this sacrament have found a sense of healing, not necessarily for the physical illness itself, but rather for their spirit. They have said that it brings a peace and acceptance that only stems from knowing that a loving God is in charge.

Not Just for Kids

Sacraments are opportunities for all of us to discover more about God. Through addressing the different intelligences and through being open to what God has to say to us in the sacraments, we are able to get a glimpse of heaven, a glimpse of what it is to be community.

Rumi, a mystical poet from Afghanistan living in the 1200s, wrote a poem entitled "With Passion." It is about the importance of passion in any encounter with God. We would do well to remember that, when we bring passion to the sacraments, we bring God.

With
Passion pray.
With passion make love.
With passion eat and drink and dance and play.
Why look like a dead fish
In this ocean
Of
God?

SEVEN

MULTIPLE INTELLIGENCES
AND THE LITURGICAL YEAR

We are cups, constantly and quietly being filled.
The trick is knowing how to tip ourselves over
and let the beautiful stuff out.

■ **RAY BRADBURY**

There is a magic in the liturgical year, a magic that helps us remember who we are, where we came from, and what went on before we graced the scene of this world. We celebrate Advent and watch as the anticipation flows into Christmas rejoicing—and then outward into that strange and mysterious time of Jesus' childhood. Lent comes next, once again bringing forth in us the events of Jesus' life and giving us pause as we march ever closer to that moment of crucifixion. But then the liturgical year hands us over to the joy of Easter and the hope that resurrection brings, with the powerful reminder at the end of the season of the presence of the Spirit always in our lives in the celebration of Pentecost.

And the church doesn't forget the fallow time, the Ordinary Time when we go through each day doing what we are called to do, without pomp or circumstance, without any surprises on the horizon except for the ones we bring to each day. It is indeed the extraordinary ordinary time.

With the use of exercises to awaken the multiple intelligences, the liturgical year can come alive, pregnant with numerous opportunities to grow in faith.

Advent

The liturgical year starts quietly, with a call to remember, to move once again into a time of waiting and anticipation. We pause to think of all we wait for in our lives, to think of the ultimate wait in returning to our God. We recall a world waiting for a savior, someone who would conquer death and give us hope. During this time, we need to tap into the absolute dependency on God that this waiting engenders, not only for ourselves but for those we teach. Many activities throughout this time will awaken the individual intelligences and will turn hearts and minds to God.

- *Advent wreath.* The traditional Advent wreath opens up all sorts of possibilities. It gives a very concrete center for our prayer during this time. It offers a ritual that harkens back to ancient times and allows for prayers to be centered on longing, repentance, waiting, and preparation. Using traditional prayers as well as prayers that are sung or danced or drawn or whatever, we are able to celebrate longing, waiting, and the darkest hour before the dawn.

- *The Jesse tree.* The Jesse tree traces the roots of Jesus' people from creation to his birth. This is an excellent way to talk about to whom we belong, from whom we came. Work with the Jesse tree might entail personal family histories as well as Jesus' family history. This serves to clarify our communal heritage through baptism—that everyone is our brother and sister. Creatively coming up with symbols for the various members of the Jesse tree awakens not only the bodily-kinesthetic but the other intelligences as well, as we look to musicians and artists, to mathematicians and writers, to scientists and ministers, and so many others who each have a part on that tree.

- *Hanukkah.* Hanukkah is a feast that occurs during Advent and is celebrated by the Jews to commemorate the victory of Israel over the Syrians and the rededication of the temple in Jerusalem. Using this celebration offers an opportunity for Christians to join with Jewish friends; it also gives us a time to rededicate ourselves and our work and home space to God. Simple traditions might include the blessing of the classroom, or conversations about how miracles occur, because, as tradition has it, there was only enough oil to keep the lamp in the temple sanctuary burning for one day; and despite this, the lamp burned for eight days, a sign of God's unwavering presence. Use this time to awaken the intelligences by talking about how oil is needed for the lamps to burn, how there are many things and people in our lives we mark as sacred, and how marking something as special can be done in many different ways.

- *Saints.* Celebrating the saints of Advent opens the door for many of the intelligences to be engaged. The Barbara branch is an old Advent custom that has the participants bring in a branch from a spring blooming bush, such as forsythia, place it in water, and wait for it to bloom, which it usually does before Christmas. This gives a sense of expectation and opens the door to discussions about Saint Barbara and other saints who "bloomed" after sometimes lying dormant. Legends tell us that St. Lucy was a saint from the early Christian era who brought food to Christians hiding from persecution. She wore lighted candles in a wreath on her hair to keep her hands free to carry the food and light the way. St. Nicholas Day, on December 6th, gives an opportunity to put Santa Claus in perspective; conversation can take place about a bishop who helped a woman because she lacked a dowry, who saved three kidnapped boys, and who punched a fellow bishop at the Council of Nicaea. Talk about opportunities for discussion and awakening the intelligences! And those are just a few of the Advent saints.

• *Household customs.* Customs from different countries offer opportunities throughout Advent to draw again on the
many intelligences. Visual-spatial, bodily-kinesthetic, musical-rhythmic, interpersonal, and intrapersonal intelligences
are engaged with Christmas card listening, where the message is perhaps used as a prayer, the card itself is discussed,
and the people who sent it are remembered. The Advent
buzzard, a German custom, has a coat hanger bent to resem-
ble a bird. It is covered in black paper and hung in a promi-
nent place. Each person who passes gives it a whack and says,
"Light overcomes darkness!" awakening the naturalist, the
interpersonal, the intrapersonal, and the bodily-kinesthetic.

Christmas

For many of us, Christmas lasts a day or a week at the most. When we
look to the liturgical year, we see that it covers from the birth of Jesus
all the way to his baptism.

Christmas celebrates the birth of our savior, the coming of he who
would teach us in the ways of God. It is the birth of he who awakened
the intelligences in us all so many years ago.

• *Las posadas.* This is an opportunity to engage all the intelligences. This is a Latin American custom that can and has
been adapted by many people in many countries. It is, in essence, the simple telling of the birth of Jesus—the journey
from inn to inn and finally finding shelter in the stable. This
simple and spontaneous drama can teach us much about re-
jection, fatigue, longing, quiet, and peace. If the invitation is
open, stories will abound about the cry of the human heart
when these emotions surface.

• *The Twelve Days of Christmas.* This well-known carol is an
excellent tool to use to awaken all of the intelligences and
new avenues of faith growth. Together, write a new version

of the song, using symbols that emphasize different items of our faith, each of which could mark one of the twelve days. The Jesse tree could give way to the God tree, with appropriate symbols for the twelve days. Whatever evolves, all will be good for strengthening the intelligences in the children in your classroom.

- *Blessing of the Christmas tree.* This blessing allows for reflection on everlasting life, the importance of growth, and the beauty of this symbol of the season. Discussion can center on the tree as a symbol of life, as a symbol of remembrance of Christmases past. Activities might include preparing a prayer service that incorporates the tree as a blessing to the group. Information about trees from those with a strong naturalist intelligence might add interesting avenues to explore during the blessing of the Christmas tree.

- *Gift giving.* Gift giving allows us to explore the different approaches to gifts. What about the gifts of time, talent, and treasure? What makes a good gift? Can a kind thought be a gift? Can a song or a dance be a gift? Activities might revolve around the gifts the Magi brought to Jesus. Do we give these kinds of gifts to people today? What was it that made the gifts of the Magi special? Address all the intelligences and ask the children about what constitutes a good gift. What would be a good gift for a logical-mathematical person? For someone strong in bodily-kinesthetic intelligence? Do people with strong intrapersonal intelligence need gifts?

- *Epiphany.* Epiphany means manifestation or showing. It is the celebration of a revelation of something greater to come. The Magi visited the child from whom great things were expected. Activities might include considering what is being manifested in our lives that hint at greater things to come. Is my interest in science and plants a hint of a future in biology? Is my interest in people a manifestation of my future work in some type of service? This is an opportunity through the intelligences to look to strengths and gifts and how they might be used in the future. We, like the Magi, are bearing gifts that we are meant to share with the world. How are we preparing?

Lent

The word *lent* is a derivative of the Old English word "lencten," which means "springtime." This is the time of the liturgical year that is full of discipline, bringing us to the springtime of our souls, which is full of spiritual renewal and growth. It aptly prepares us for the celebration of Easter. It is during this time that we should become more aware of the fact that we are not to worry; instead, we are to trust in a loving Father for all we need. It is a time when we need to remember that we are called to find God in everything and everyone around us.

- *Lenten symbols.* The symbols of the season present a good opportunity to awaken multiple intelligences. Colors are full of symbolism and awaken the visual-spatial intelligences along many avenues: what the colors signify, what sorrow, purity, growth, and joy look like. The bare branch, the butterfly, and seeds are vivid symbols for the naturalist intelligence. Using the symbols of salt, oil, and water opens the door for the interpersonal and intrapersonal intelligences to determine the implications for community and self-growth. The music of the season appeals to the musical-rhythmic intelligence through the pronounced cadence of repentance and sorrow. The Stations of the Cross, the seven wounds of Jesus, and the forty days of Lent all speak to the logical-mathematical intelligence.

- *Stations of the Cross* can be used in many different ways. They can be rewritten with either a modern theme or with a theme that calls to mind our baptism or one that addresses the major struggles of life. Get inside the feelings of the people one encounters in the stations. Can you imagine what they were thinking, what they were feeling? Try putting the stations to music, with each station having a unique song to portray the essence of what was taking place.

• *Fasting* can be an opportunity to grow during Lent. This doesn't have to be from food; although, if it is, carry it out to a concrete finish, such as showing the one who fasted for one day a week during Lent how much money could go to feed someone experiencing real hunger. Explore together what other ways there are to fast, such as from a favorite game or from a favorite activity. In what ways can our tongues "fast" during Lent? In what ways can our minds "fast" during Lent? All of these avenues address the multiple intelligences.

• *Saints.* Looking to lenten saints is another way to bring this liturgical season alive. St. Patrick's Day arrives during Lent. Talk about how the shamrock was used to teach the Trinity, how people wore green around this time to celebrate springtime and to celebrate that people separated from the church were returning. Consider what types of struggles St. Patrick encountered talking about faith. How do we struggle with talking about our faith? St. Joseph, the foster father of Jesus, reminds us that every person has a unique job in the history of salvation. The special custom of the St. Joseph's table is practiced to celebrate Joseph's job as a carpenter, with the best of meatless foods spread out to give to the poor, lonely, and hungry people. What is our place in the salvation story? What special gift can I give to the community? How do we as a community reach out to the poor, as St. Joseph did?

• *Almsgiving* is a good topic to address during Lent. The

word "alms" comes from the Greek word for "compassion." With compassion we try to feel what someone else is feeling. When we introduce almsgiving into the classroom, we can talk about where the money goes, why it is best done in secret, and why it should be done daily in some way, shape, or form so that our compassion for others will grow. Such a practice in the classroom, even outside of Lent, awakens the best in all the intelligences.

• *The paschal meal* is a Christian adaptation of the Passover. Within the ritual is the main part of the Passover—the story of the Israelites' escape from Egypt—but added are some of the key points Jesus made at the Last Supper. This formal dinner offers to the different intelligences opportunities to explore the history and the impact of those last words of Jesus. Many available resources exist, but it is not wrong to create your own paschal meal, written, acted out, and sung by your children.

• *Holy Week* is overflowing with possibilities for growth in faith: Palm Sunday and the triumphant journey; the waiting in the early part of the week, knowing what is to happen; the Thursday meal that carries so many lessons; the sorrow of Friday; the loneliness of Saturday. All of these give ample opportunity for us to bring those incidents to life for our students.

Easter

For Easter, the biggest celebration of the liturgical year, we woefully lack in celebrating. The church proclaims that the Easter season extends for 50 days, but very little energy is carried through in the celebration of Jesus Christ, the Son of God, rising from the dead and giving us new life and reason to hope. From early Christian days and, in fact, up to the early 1900s, long Easter celebrations abounded. Granted, this celebration often sprang from a realization of mortality, which loomed because of high infant death rates and short life spans. Today with modern medicine giving us longer lives, often disease free, we forget the message of the resurrection and lapse back into our routine of daily life. Getting that message across and keeping that celebration alive is a challenge worth meeting.

- *Rogation days* were a regular celebration in times gone by. These days were special days of blessing and dedication of the fields to God. The days following Easter Sunday give us an opportunity to talk about the new life and to dedicate our "fields" to growing something. Whether that be in a planter or in a dedicated space around the church, create a solemn blessing, a definite ritual for the planting, and assignments for the care and harvesting. Those with the naturalist intelligence will rejoice in this activity—as will many with bodily-kinesthetic (in the act of planting) and logical-mathematical (in figuring the spaces needed for the plants) intelligences.

- *Emmaus walk.* Institute an Emmaus walk, which can be done in any space, for any length of time. The simplicity of it is that you take the students and go for a walk with the simple admonition to "come and see." Talk about everything you see—new plants sprouting, people refurbishing with paint or raking the garden, cars getting washed—and tie it back to the resurrection. Not only does such an activity build a God mind-set; it also has all of the intelligences processing the meaning of resurrection.

- *Dyngus* is a custom of Polish origin that I had the good fortune to grow up with. Dyngus occurred on the Monday and Tuesday after Easter. On Monday the boys tried to surprise the girls with a spray of water to remind them of their baptism. On Tuesday the ritual was repeated with the girls surprising the boys. It was a light-hearted ritual that conjured up the fact that we are all family because of our baptism, that we are all entitled to share in this new life together. A variation of Dyngus in your classroom might be sprinkling each other with water while talking about our baptisms and what it means to be a member of this community. Again, many of the intelligences are brought into play. It is also a good opportunity to remind the students of the newly baptized in the parish and to discuss what we can do for them to help them grow in their faith.

- *The Ascension* can be celebrated in many ways. Perhaps you have a candle burning in your room to remind each other of God's presence. Extinguish the candle near the Ascension and talk about what that means. Do activities that involve "ascending," like rising to the occasion to help a person in need, rising to become all God made us to be, rising to new heights of knowledge and exercise of faith. Engage the intelligences to come up with new ideas to celebrate Jesus' ascension into heaven.

Pentecost

Pentecost is the church's celebration of the gift of the Holy Spirit. You might say it is the celebration of the birth of God's very life and energy in us. What happens when people allow the Spirit to work in them is shown in the fruits of love, joy, peace, patience, kindness, goodness, faithfulness, gentleness, and self-control. It is the Spirit we need when we work with children in a religious education classroom and when we work with adults in any setting. We have to trust the Spirit to work in and through us, and we need to be open to the Spirit manifested in the people around us. What a fitting celebration for multiple intelligences! We have to trust the Spirit when we are the catechist—most especially if we are going to use activities in our presentations that allow multiple intelligences to grow.

- *Fly kites.* Make use of kites for a symbol of the Spirit. Fly the kites and discuss what the kite needs to fly—cooperation from the kite handler, a good wind, freedom from obstacles such as power lines. What parallels can be drawn between the kite and the Spirit? Are we the kite or the kite operator? Bring in the bodily-kinesthetic and visual-spatial intelligence by designing a "Spirit" kite. Test it in the field.

- *Gifts are from the Spirit.* Engage the interpersonal and intrapersonal intelligences by looking at the different gifts of the Spirit and seeing how they are manifested in people. Consider the gifts of the people in the classroom and determine what gifts of the Spirit are used with those gifts. Could there be other gifts we are not aware of? Paul's list of gifts wasn't meant to be all-inclusive—just what was commonly recognized at the time. What other gifts might be considered gifts of the Spirit? Celebrate individual gifts in creative ways—ways that get each of the intelligences to shine.

- *Birthday symbols* can be used to celebrate Pentecost. Make a cake together and then talk about the symbols of a birthday—the candles marking each year, the celebration with family and friends, the gifts, the special music for the day. In addition to these, how can we celebrate the greatness of what is to come, especially for the community of the church?

Ordinary Time

Ordinary Time reminds me of summer when I was growing up. On the last day of school the summer stretched before us like a gift of surprises full of lazy and crazy days, with time to run and play and just be. Ordinary Time in the church is like that—a celebration of the ordinary yet extraordinary things of life. It calls us to see the surprises in daily life and to respond to the "aha!" moments that are hiding in each day.

- *"Aha!" moments* are good to share with one another. It might be something as simple as realizing that getting up in the early morning is a special time. Other "aha!" moments may carry deeper significance. Whatever the moment, take some time not just to share it, but to talk about how to sharpen eyes and ears so that we are open to those moves of the Spirit. The intrapersonal and the existential intelligence will thrive on this type of sharing as it continues to give insight into what life is all about as well as our place in it.

- *Centering prayer.* Ordinary Time is a good time to introduce centering prayer. Show how an ordinary statement such as "God is love" can be an opportunity for great things to happen, through breathing in and breathing out and repeating the phrase. Be sure to talk about the insights gleaned and the difficulty of such a prayer time. If the centering prayer is concentrating on the in-out of breathing, you will be incorporating all of the intelligences.

- *Ordinary activities.* Leaf gathering, pumpkin cutting, apple picking are all ordinary activities that can bring us to a greater appreciation of this Ordinary Time in the church calendar. Talk together about the different daily activities of the summer as it moves into fall and how those activities bring us in contact with God. Gather leaves; explore one leaf; make leaf prints; draw your own leaf; make up a song for the leaves of fall; dance a dance of change of summer into fall; contemplate the birth and death cycle—all of these will engage the intelligences in the very ordinary time of the church.

Ordinary Time is, paraphrasing Thich Nhat Hanh, a Buddhist monk, a time not to look for miracles such as walking on water or curing a blind man; rather, it is a time to realize that every day we are knee-deep in miracles.

Not Just for Kids

Using ritual during the liturgical year is not just for kids. Rituals will awaken the intelligences of all people, enabling them to look at their faith in a holistic way. Rituals engage the whole person, calling them to remember that there is a definite cycle of life and death and rebirth in which we all have a part.

By following the liturgical year, we catechists are able to address all the intelligences with the children and adults with whom we work. We can celebrate the important times that take us so well through the cycle of life, helping us to wait and celebrate, to suffer and to mourn, to rejoice and to hope, to reach out to others and to remember that the ordinary times make up the bulk of life and our relationship with our God, and that it is all good.

EIGHT

MULTIPLE INTELLIGENCES
AND PERSONAL SPIRITUALITY

*Wonder encourages us to stand humbly before
the unfathomable mysteries of human life, trusting
that, in them, we encounter God.*

■ **MELANNIE SVOBODA**

We catechists have people under our care for a small portion of their lives. For some, our encounter with them lasts a mere sixty minutes out of a week and only twenty-eight of the fifty-two weeks in the year. For others, our encounters might be increased by involvement in vacation church offerings, special activities throughout the year, or contact with individuals for various reasons. Such limited involvement points to the importance of helping those we encounter develop their own spirituality, their own relationship with a God who will be with them through their lifetime and beyond.

Bill Peet, a writer of children's books, tells the story of Chester the worldly pig. Chester wanted so much to leave the farm. He felt deep down that he wasn't really meant to be a pig, living day after day in muck and mayhem, and above all he didn't want to become bacon. He thought he must have some talent, some gift that would take him away from the pigpen. When he saw that a circus was coming through town, he started practicing standing on his nose, convinced that a pig standing on his nose would be an attraction. It was, but only if that pig was surrounded by tigers. When Chester fainted during the performance, he was relegated to being a clown's sidekick and, through a series of misadventures, ended up dodging trouble in the city. Reluctantly, he decided that becoming bacon was his fate. When a carnival promoter passed through town, he discovered Chester and the wonderful map of the world on his side formed by his own beautiful spots. Chester had his gift with him the entire time. He just had to recognize it in himself.

We catechists want to make sure that the talent, the gift, and the faith that are each individual child's can shine. We want each child to continue to develop that faith, discovering the unique talents and gifts that are very much a part of each of them. Just as Chester's special talent was part of him, so too we have something very special to offer to the community around us and to ourselves. We have many special gifts, manifest in the many intelligences, and we only have to open up our eyes. Sometimes those eyes don't open because we forget that God is at work in our lives.

The story is told of Abraham, who had difficulty understanding what God meant when God spoke about Abraham leading a nation of people. Abraham wondered who these people would be. Would he be able to lead these people? God obviously was seeing talents that Abraham wasn't. Can you just imagine the struggle Abraham went through just after talking with God?

> The man paced back and forth, his hands pulling at his hair. He laughed to himself.
>
> "Heir! Ha! Heir! Yahweh said I would have heirs that number more than the stars." He grimaced. "More than the stars?" He shook his head. " I can't lead a nation of people."
>
> He felt a nudge and turned. Nothing. Unless...Unless it was Yahweh reminding him to trust, to be aware of his gifts.
>
> But a nation of people? He was only a herder. How was he supposed to build a nation? He was old. His bones ached. He was tired. AND he couldn't even have a single

solitary heir of his own. He glanced over at the sleeping form across the room. Sarah, old like him and unable to bear a child. He was so afraid she was going to be a bitter old woman. And if that were true, what kind of nation would take kindly to two old and bitter people?

Quietly he pulled aside the tent flap. The night was also quiet, the sky clear. Abraham looked up. Thousands of stars twinkled back at him. "A nation that would number more than the stars." He squinted as he studied the stars more closely. Different. Each different. Some so small, some shining with such brilliance. He watched as one star shot across the sky, its light dying quickly into the dark. Will this nation be like the stars? he thought. Will there be people who will be part of the nation but work behind the scenes, working each day, loving, being, doing nothing extraordinary but shining just the same? Would there be leaders who would take responsibility after he died? Would they lead with compassion and love?

He jumped as an owl's cry cut into the stillness. He touched the dagger in his belt. How many would attack this nation of people? Who would hate this nation? Who would this nation hate? Who would this nation love?

Another star shot across the sky, its brilliance lighting the sky for a brief moment and then fading into darkness. How would he handle those who had the gifts, the talents, the intelligence, but refused to use the gifts for the good of the nation?

Abraham paused. Nation? Yes, a nation but really a family, a people who looked to Yahweh for strength and guidance.

As another noise came to his ears, his hand once more tightened around his dagger. He tensed every muscle ready to defend his home and family. The rustle grew louder and Abraham crouched, ready to spring.

Suddenly he started to laugh as a duck and her babies walked out of the bush and across the yard. A nation of people who would be afraid of ducks! A huge smile crossed Abraham's face. Maybe he could run a nation. Maybe if he trusted in God, he would have whatever he needed. Maybe things would be okay. He stretched and yawned, and smiled as he went inside. He slipped off his sandals and got into bed, trying not to disturb Sarah. He needn't have worried. Sarah turned to face him. "Couldn't sleep?"

Abraham nodded, reaching out to stroke her graying hair. "I was wondering if I could lead the nation Yahweh spoke of."

Sarah laughed. "You worry about that? God will give you the strength and wisdom." She tugged at his beard. "Better you should worry if you'll be a good father."

Abraham's drooping eyelids shot open. "A good father?"

Sarah giggled as if she were 16. "Yes, a good father."

Abraham couldn't get the words out. "Father? You mean...you mean you are with child?"

Sarah nodded. "Yes. You are going to be a father."

This story about developing spirituality raises many questions. When have you been afraid like Abraham? When have you questioned God's ability to work in your life? How have you been surprised by God as Abraham was? What nation do you feel a part of? How do you react to giving your life over to God? What frightens you about trusting God? What renews your spirit? How are you like Abraham? What kind of star are you?

By taking time with your students to explore these questions, you are taking time to help them explore their personal spirituality. And oftentimes this gives you time to explore your own.

One of the best ways for you as well as your students to explore spirituality is to utilize the twelve steps used by addiction programs worldwide. The twelve steps are great stepping-off points for looking at our relationship with God and with others, with many opportunities to develop our spirituality. The different intelligences are addressed, and the steps are wide open to innovation and creativity. In other words, the twelve steps can help in the developing of spirituality in our children and ourselves.

The first step says: "We admitted we were powerless over our addiction—that our lives had become unmanageable." This is a most important step in spirituality—admitting that we cannot do anything alone. Consider some of the possible questions to pose when talking about this step. When are the times we are powerless over something? What gets in the way when we try to control a situation? How are our lives affected? By discussing the first step as it addresses our faith development, we find that we are powerless over our lives. We need God.

That leads into the second step, which reads: "We came to believe that a Power greater than ourselves could restore us to sanity." This is the acknowledgement of the Higher Power, of God and our need for God. Questions that could arise out of this step might be any of the following: When have we felt that a power greater than ourselves could restore us to sanity? What other ways have we tried to restore our sanity? How are our lives affected? By grappling with the need for someone greater than ourselves to help us grow, to become the best we can be, we are able to move forward in our spiritual journey by turning our lives over to God as talked about in the third step.

The third step reads: "We made a decision to turn our will and our lives over to the care of God as we understood God." This step delightfully opens us up to discussing together our image of God and what type of relationship we have with God. How do I understand God? What keeps me from turning my life to God? In what instance have I turned my life over to God, and what resulted?

When we move to step four—"We made a searching and fearless moral inventory of ourselves"—we are ready to look at ourselves, both the good and bad sides, and see where we need God's help the most. Questions might include: When was the last time I took an inventory of myself? When people say we are as sick as our secrets, what do they mean? When we take an inventory of ourselves, do we only consider what we perceive is "wrong" with us? When dealing with spirituality, this step allows us to recognize our gifts as well as our failings. It calls us to honesty and helps us to acknowledge our total person.

The fifth step is difficult. In this step, we "admit to God, to ourselves, and to another human being the exact nature of our wrongs." This addresses our need for reconciliation. The forgiveness we receive from another helps our relationship with God and with the community. Questions to consider might be: What happens in our lives when we admit that we have done wrong to another? What does the phrase "the truth shall make us free" mean in the context of this step?

The sixth step is: "We were entirely ready to have God remove all these defects of character." This calls us to open ourselves to God's work in our lives. We are willing to endure what it takes to help us grow, even if that is difficult or painful for us. This step ties closely with the seventh step, in which "we humbly asked God to remove our shortcomings." You could say that the seventh step is a commitment to growth, a willingness to change so growth can take place. Questions to consider for these steps might include: What are some of the things in me that need God's help? What will help me be ready for the changes in me that will take place when I ask God to remove my shortcomings? What am I most afraid of when it comes to changing?

The next two steps take place over time and cannot be taken lightly. Discussion about these steps is essential if growth in the Spirit is to take place. The eighth and ninth steps are: "We made a list of all persons we had harmed and became willing to make amends to them all," and "We made direct amends to such people wherever possible, except when to do so would injure them or others." The last part of the ninth step is most important and means more discussion about when making amends will be hurtful. What are some of these situations? Why would this be important to act on? How does God play a part in making amends?

The tenth, eleventh, and twelfth steps are a series of commitment to growth. In the tenth step, "We continued to take personal inventory and when we were wrong promptly admitted it."

The eleventh step gives us a way of continuing to stay in touch with our Higher Power because "we sought through prayer and meditation to improve our conscious contact with God, as we understood God, praying only for knowledge of God's will for us and the power to carry that out." Things to consider are: What are the ways in which I as an individual can grow? How do I grow with the community? What is my commitment to prayer? How can I use my unique intelligences to grow?

The last step, the twelfth, is: "Having had a spiritual awakening as the result of these steps, we tried to carry this message to those addicted to something and to practice these principles in all our affairs." It could read, "Having had a spiritual awakening as a result of these encounters, we try to love those around us no matter what, and to practice in all our affairs the guidance God gives us." This outreach to the community is so important to spiritual growth. This is the evangelization of each other. It is the willingness to share what our faith is and how our religion helps us to grow. It calls upon us to use our own intelligences as well as to help awaken the intelligences in the community, recognizing always that God guides our hand.

Personal spirituality is difficult. We as catechists are called to help those in our charge grow in their faith so that no matter what religious path they choose in their adult lives, their relationship with God will be solid and ever-growing.

NINE

WHEN YOU TAKE THE
LEAP OF FAITH WITH THE SPIRIT

In the end these things matter most:
How well did you love? How fully did you
live? How deeply did you learn to let go?

■ **THE BUDDHA**

T hroughout this book we have been looking at ways in which we can help our children grow. I have offered approaches that use the multiple intelligences present in the classroom to awaken the Spirit in each of us. I could go on and tell stories catechists have told me about the surprises and blessings that occurred in their classrooms when the multiple intelligences were addressed. Instead, I will tell you one story that has no children in it.

I was leading a retreat for religious educators in the diocese of Erie, Pennsylvania. The retreat focused on prayer and the multiple intelligences. We began with an introduction to the theory of multiple intelligences and then moved on to how knowledge of this theory could be used in prayer.

We talked about what the right prayer is for each individual and about expectations in prayer. We did several of the exercises I do with children, and we took some time for individual prayer.

When we gathered again, we considered what it is to have a mindset of God, a state of mind in which God's presence just permeates everything. When we look at peanut butter we see God as a staple in our lives; we see the importance of "sticking" with God. We know that, like peanuts, which grow underground, God is always, even if silent, working in our lives.

Toward the end of the evening, after experiencing the different intelligences in action, I gave each small group an intelligence along with the instruction to create a prayer to share with the entire group. They were to remember that there is no one right or wrong way to pray, and they were to apply the intelligence and prepare to pray the prayer before the whole group.

I was shaking in my boots wondering what would happen. I watched as each group worked away. I answered any questions, but gave very few suggestions. Finally, the prayer began.

It opened with a Scripture reading, which the group did in a stand-up-and-read theatre style so that the word was literally coming at us from all over the room. This moved into a beautiful mathematical problem that was solved by the group and pointed to the steadiness of God's presence. We were asked by the visual-spatial group to close our eyes and imagine a world without God, and then, when we were touched on our shoulders, to take our minds into a different direction by picturing a world with God. The intrapersonal group wrote on the board, "Who is God to you?" After a few moments of silence, a litany of who God is rang through the room. "Giver of life. Lord and Savior. Provider. Wise One. Cornerstone. Compassionate One."

As the voices faded, the interpersonal group stood and asked us to greet those on either side of us, then to become quiet, and, finally, to look into the eyes of the other and see God present. The naturalist group then stood, each one coming forth with a flower, creating a bouquet while offering up the petitions of the group. This bouquet of petitions was offered with solemn ceremony both to the heavens and to the community in prayer. The musical group started with a chant that moved into a familiar hymn and ended in a modern-day song. The bodily-kinesthetic group asked the musical group to repeat their songs, and gradually they invited all to dance as one, praising God and remembering the community we have in each other. Finally, the existential group called us to remember that God is our source and our life and that God is manifest through us as we love and support one another. The prayer ended with a large group hug.

Such a prayer I have never experienced. The presence of God in community was felt so keenly. Many people expressed thoughts on the power of the experience, and the director said afterward that "this experience has generated an incredible sense of community and camaraderie."

All was generated by the Spirit, by using various activities to address all the intelligences. We were using these activities with adults, though they are used more regularly with children. Adults in their own way benefit far more than children from having all the intelligences addressed. It is almost as if a hunger is operating in their lives, a hunger for creativity, for expression, for God to be manifest in their lives. Addressing the different intelligences allows the adults to experience once again the power and beauty of God.

Using the multiple intelligences approach in adult formation calls for courage. Adults are not used to different ways of learning. Many have forgotten their creativity; many have forgotten that their bodies are as much a part of them as their spirit; many feel that only traditional prayer and solemn actions are what God desires of them.

The first thing to do when applying multiple intelligences to adult faith formation classes is to get out of the traditional box. Because your parish has been doing adult religious education the same way for many years does not mean that it has to continue that way. Think of new approaches that would be possible. Might the adults want to meet as families? Would they enjoy a historical lesson on a particular Bible passage? Would they gain a different insight by acting out the story of the Good Samaritan instead of just listening to the word? Might different approaches to prayer be a need for your adults?

When you do embark on getting out of the box that adult learning has often been restricted to, expect resistance—resistance from the people who are reluctant to give up their comfort zone, resistance from the pastor who doesn't want to deal with questions that might arise from the new approach, resistance from the "Old Faithful" members who keep saying, "We've always done it this way." When all of this happens, remember the old saying: "The only person who likes change is a wet baby." Remember also that change is inevitable, and everyone resists change.

When you do decide to change your approach to adult formation, you might be surprised to find that you are devoid of ideas. This results from the fact that the more we do something in the same way, the more difficult it will be to think about changing, to consider doing something in a totally different way. The best way to deal with this is to break out of your own patterns. Put your clothes on in a different order. Maybe you always put your socks on first. Save them for last. If you put your pants on before your shirt, reverse that order. By doing these small things you will find that you are able to think in a different way, to break free of the restraints that have been so ingrained in your life and in your approach to adult formation.

Pablo Picasso, the great artist, said: "Every child is an artist. The problem is how to remain an artist when you grow up." He was speaking about how many adults stop their dreaming, their creativity, their imagining, once they become "adult." Creativity studies show a great spike in creativity and imagination in kindergarten and first grade. However, that spike turns into a downward spiral around the second and third grade as children learn through subtle messages that creativity is not something that is carried into adulthood. We end up with a large group of adults who have forgotten about fairy tales, storytelling, and make-believe. That loss shuts the door on the Spirit, who works through our creativity and imagination.

If you are serious about bringing a vibrant faith to the adults you work with, go though the rest of this book and insert "adult," "participant," or "seeker" into the text everywhere the words "child," "student," or "kids" appear. All of these activities are activities that can and should be used with adults. We need to reawaken the child in each of us. And when that child is awakened, be prepared to offer many different ways for that creativity and imagination to grow. Be ready to introduce the participants to an ever-changing, ever-surprising, ever-creative God.

Introducing the idea of multiple intelligences to a group of adults is indeed daunting. Reassure them that, for the time together, everyone can experience what is happening together. When everyone heads home, each person can determine what was liked and what wasn't liked, what was comfortable and what was uncomfortable. Instruct them that once they are home they need to look at the experience. Urge them to consider what they enjoyed and what they didn't and why, and what tugged at a little something in the heart. As an adult, you might not like all the activities; you might squirm at some, but if you experience them, you will find that some address a very real need in you both for your growth and your relationship with God.

Growth in faith, discovering more and more about God each day, is what we are called to live. We have to always be open to new ways of learning about God, new ways that will open up our minds to all the different possibilities God might bring into our lives. Whether we are learners or teachers, as adults we need to be open to all that God can teach us. What better example for our children?

For people of faith, God is a supreme creator who loved us into existence and loves us through life, ever ready to support and hold us whenever we are in need. This God is the God to hang with, the God who will see us through anything, the God who will be with us no matter our choices, the God of multiple intelligences who, in wisdom, shares those intelligences with us and calls us to love each other. We can love each other in unique ways, whether child or adult, because we have those intelligences gifted to us by an all-knowing and all-loving and all-intelligent God.

APPENDIX

I don't know where my ideas come from.
They just come usually when I'm mowing the
lawn, driving to work, or walking my hound.

■ **RON KOFRON**

Working with the theory of multiple intelligences, you may find that you are developing your creativity as you seek ways in which to appeal to the different intelligences in your classroom. You will find your mind discovering new and different ways to look at an idea, and you will soon find out that creativity is at every turn.

I have included here a potpourri of activities. I have deliberately not labeled them with an intelligence so as to keep away from making it appear that some activities appeal to one or two intelligences and not the others.

Also, each of these activities can be adapted for various subjects that arise in the religious education classroom. With a simple addition or different approach, something centered on baptism might easily be usable for a lenten class.

In any event, relax and let the Spirit work right along with you.

Word cartoons

In this particular activity, words and pictures team together so both the linguistic and the visual intelligences get some exercise. In each cartoon the word is an important part of the drawing. The exercise could be used with any subject and serves as reinforcement for key concepts. To make a word cartoon, pick a word and try to make that into a picture. The pictures will not necessarily be great works of art, but the exercise will stretch the mind to consider interesting possibilities about the word.

Drawing the fine line
Choose a particular word. Now, without lifting your pencil, draw that word. If the word is "sacrament," the picture might illustrate how all the sacraments are connected, how the *s* flows into the *a* and the *a* climbs to the *c* and so on. The exercise is made all the more challenging as there should be only the start point and the endpoint in the picture.

Washing us clean
You will need a cutting board, a large soft bar of floating soap un-wrapped for 24 hours, a plastic knife, a stainless steel dinner knife.

Use the plastic knife to scrape away the soap's brand name. Then think of a symbol that represents the cleaning power of baptism or reconciliation or forgiveness. Trace the drawing onto the soap. Place the soap on the cutting board and cut out the design using the stain-less steel dinner knife. Cut the soap from top to bottom.

To shape the cut-out symbol, hold the symbol in your hand and carve it with the plastic knife. Work on one section of the symbol at a time. Use the plastic knife to put in details and finally smooth the finished carving with your fingers or a tissue.

Balloon animals
Help the children to make balloon animals. Books abound about the balloon technique, and this technique does not have to be perfect. The children will be creating animals, but they will run into problems when balloons break or the animal doesn't come out as they wish. After ev-eryone has had an opportunity to make an animal (or something sim-pler if animals seem overwhelming), discuss the difficulty of creating and the joy of making something. Take some time to thank God for the gift of creation.

Passover celebration

The Jewish festival of freedom called the Passover celebrates the flight of the Jewish people from Egypt, where they were slaves. Haroses, a traditional food, symbolizes the mortar that holds the stones together and that was used to build structures for the Egyptians.

Recipe for haroses: 1 medium-size apple, ½ cup of shelled walnuts, ¼ teaspoon ground cinnamon, dash of ground ginger, 3 tablespoons of grape juice. Wash and peel the apple. Chop it into small pieces and put the pieces in a medium-size bowl. Chop the walnuts into tiny pieces with a nut chopper or a knife. Mix the nuts, cinnamon, ginger, and grape juice with the apples. Spoon the mixture into a serving bowl. Spread haroses on pieces of matzo.

The beauty of creation

You will need magnifying glasses of various sizes and strengths. Talk about the magnifying glasses, and solicit ideas from the children as to what magnifying glasses are. Talk about how God created the world and how a lot of the time we don't really see creation. Have a collection of rocks, leaves, flowers, and other objects from nature. The children should have sufficient time to really examine the items. Talk about the differences between just looking and looking with the magnifying glass. Bring it back to a discussion of what a wondrous gift is creation.

Taking it further might include drawing an object first, then examining it with the magnifying glass and adding additional details. Talk about how to keep our eyes open always to creation.

The loving support of God

You will need a clear plastic jar, water, red or blue vegetable dye (food coloring), and a bunch of fresh, crisp celery with leaves attached.

Show the children the celery and talk about how the celery was grown and cut. Give each child a celery stick to examine. Explain how the plants need water to survive, and find out what the children know about how a plant gets the water to survive. Talk about how we are like the plants, how we need water—God—to grow to become all we were meant to be. Ask the children if they would like to see how plants get water to stay alive and healthy.

Partially fill the jar with water. Add enough food coloring to give the water a dark color. Snap the bottom off the celery sticks and place them immediately in the water. Soon the children will see the water moving up the plant. Have a discussion about how we receive help from God—through others, through prayer, through time with God—and how it changes us.

Where are the seeds? Where is the growth?

You will need bananas, strawberries, kiwi fruit, sharp knife, plastic knives, magnifying glass.

Show the fruit to the children. Ask where the seeds might be. Cut across the fruit. Do they see any seeds? Slice the banana crosswise and give it to the children, asking them to find the seeds. Use a magnifying glass for closer examination. Talk about how we have the capability to grow just like seeds. Sometimes we have to search for the seeds of growth in ourselves, but they are there. God gives us the potential to grow, no matter the size of our seeds.

Mixed nuts—an exercise in similarities and differences

You will need a bag of mixed nuts, kitchen tongs, a basket large enough to hold the nuts, and containers for as many of the nut varieties as you have.

Show the children how to use the tongs and then ask them to sort the nuts according to kind. When they finish, talk about the similarities and differences. How is this carried out in God's family?

Create a parade to celebrate a sacrament

Plan a parade with your students. Make some floats, have a marching band made of instruments from the classroom, and have famous dignitaries from the Scriptures. These will all be part of the parade. All the materials in the parade should have some symbolic connection to faith.

Growing story

Start a story in your classroom that will take you through the year. The story will bring home the different faith aspects that are being dealt with in your classroom. Additions can be made by you or the kids, and the story is told from week to week. Make notes for yourself so you will remember the story line.

Faith collage

Using different materials, have each child create a collage of what type of person of faith they will be like when they get older. Having them think about their faith in the future is a good way to keep that faith alive after the classroom.

Exploring other religions

For the different occurrences in the liturgical year, have the students research a similar celebration that occurs in other religions. Talk together about how faith joins us and how religion helps individuals learn about God.

Music time

Incorporate different types of music into your time together. Create a song to celebrate our faith. Have each student make an instrument that is like them (perhaps a kazoo for a down-to-earth person or a harp for a person who enjoys the nuances of life), and create a song to celebrate our unique creation from God.

Builders for God

For one class have the children build fences or forts or other buildings that they have to "protect" or which separate them from one another. Insert some situation, such as a tornado striking the town. How do the people in the different "structures" act?

We are all in this together and yet unique

Do group drawings. Talk beforehand about how we are each unique with different gifts from God. Each person starts a drawing and, after three minutes, passes it on to another. Discuss, afterward, the pluses and minuses of working together with each other's gifts.

Letter time
Each student should write a letter to someone in the class. Make sure each person will be getting a letter. Have the students consider what gift the person they are writing to has, and then have them write a letter using only pictures to let the person know what gift is appreciated. There should be at least three pictures (or more, depending on the age) to each letter.

Exploring songs
Choose a song. This might be a popular song, a church hymn, or even a nursery rhyme song. Have everyone get comfortable and listen to the song. Then together determine what this says about God, community, faith.

Memory book
Do a joint memory book for your class. Take pictures throughout the year and attach the pictures to a page in a scrapbook. Have the students write stories and prayers for each picture.

Stories of faith
Clip pictures from magazines, and keep the pictures in a box or bag. When it is time to consider how faith is working in people's lives, pull out four or five pictures and put them in a random order and have the class tell a story about what they see, especially as faith is operating or not operating in the people's lives.

Working as a community
Take a grocery bag and fill it with five or ten random items. Have the class (or small groups) work together to create a new community invention that will help foster unity and draw the community closer to-

gether. Working with the random objects to invent something helps build community as well.

Faith connections

Begin at the start of the year by introducing a long string and a box of buttons. Place a button on the string. Tell the children that the button is to represent the faith experience of coming together to learn more about God and the community. Each time someone in the class can make a connection to faith and what draws people together, they add a unique button to the chain.

Building blocks

Keep a basket of blocks in your room, no matter the age group, and use them at times to illustrate some of the lessons taking place. Use your creativity and the creativity of the children in your classroom to make this happen.

Real life

Cut pictures from the daily newspaper, or print pictures from the Internet. Have the children tell the story of what happened before and what happened after the moment caught in a photo. Talk about how this could be different with faith or how faith made this outcome possible.

Alphabet

Assign each person in the class a different letter of the alphabet. Throughout the class, come up with as many words as they can that begin with the letter and that relate to the day's lesson.

Putting the lesson to music

Pick out a song that conveys the theme of the class. Have either individuals or groups create and perform an interpretative dance to the music.

Connections
Take an opening paragraph from a book. Together read the paragraph and talk about the possible connections the class has to the paragraph. After the discussion, have the class write a story that begins with this paragraph and then continues. The final story should emphasize some aspect of faith.

Part of creation
Take some time as a group to image how some fruits came to be. Be as wild as you can, making sure that God as Creator is part of the story.

Food Like God
Use some familiar foods from the kitchen or fast food restaurants. Challenge the students to think of ways in which those foods are like God.

Recipe time
Create different recipes for living—how to be a good parent, how to keep in touch with God, how to love someone you hate. Make sure to include the measurements for all the ingredients.

Community life
Let each child have a turn planning a performance of what a Christian community is like. Make sure that they have specific scenarios to demonstrate how the community follows Jesus.

Surviving as a Christian
Have each child create a survival shoebox of items they feel are important to living a Christian life. Some items might be a Bible, or a piece of paper and pencil so that a list could be made of people to pray for, or perhaps a flute so as to sing the praises of God. Urge everyone to think as creatively as possible so that the survival shoebox will be of great help.

The Presence of God

On a beautiful day, take the students outside and spread out a blanket. Have them sit or lie, whichever is most comfortable, and just spend time together without speaking, just drinking in the surroundings. When you return to the classroom, talk about what they saw, heard, thought. See if anyone felt that God was present.

Faith recall

If you have been working on a particular theme, read the Scripture to the children once more and then ask how much they can remember of what you have been doing together. You can also do this immediately following an activity, in order to help them build up their observations and to remember what is communicated in a particular lesson.

Why class

Have a "Why" class. Begin with asking the "why" question. Perhaps it might be "Why is the Bible a book we look to for guidance?" or "Why was Jesus born in Bethlehem?" Together have the class brainstorm all the possibilities, sometimes even laughing at some of the answers. Then consider which of the brainstormed answers are perhaps the best ones.

Going beyond

When you have a particular Scripture story, have the children go beyond the story by imagining what happened next. This helps to bring the Scripture people alive.

Differences

Have the students consider differences in a unique way. Take an everyday object—perhaps a rubber band—and have them consider what an ant or bee might use the object for (for example, a swimming pool edge to confine a puddle) and then consider the other side: what might a whale use a rubber band for. Then move the conversation into the world and how there are differences in beliefs and approaches to God.

Walking a labyrinth

Make use of a labyrinth. It doesn't have to be a large outside one. You can print finger labyrinths off the Internet or have the students doodle, not lifting their pencils off the page. Call time, and then challenge them to go from the first pencil stroke to the last, using only their finger to trace the way. Talk about labyrinths as a way of centering, of becoming more aware of God.

Internet explore

For a project that is particularly good with adults, consider how life has changed with the advent of the Internet. Have a discussion about what has changed for the good, and what has changed for the not-so-good. How can we resurrect the things that are good that we have lost? How can we celebrate the things we are now able to do? What implications does this have for developing countries?

What if?

Play the "What If" game. What if the Israelites stayed in Egypt? What if Christianity never went outside of Palestine? What if Jesus had been born a woman? What if Adam and Eve had not eaten of the forbidden fruit? Talk about decisions and the impact those decisions can have on the community.

Shadow play

Figure out what you would need to make shadows of many of the symbols used by the church or in the sacraments or during the liturgical year. Use your hands or cardboard cutouts or whatever is at your disposal. Take it a step further and create a shadow play that teaches something about any of these areas.

Playing with eternity

Ask the students to draw a tree with straight lines. Each time a branch is drawn, tell them to draw three smaller branches from it. Then tell them to draw still smaller branches from each of those. Draw three twigs from each very small branch. Add roots, and do the same process again. Let them go on following the same pattern until they get tired or run out of paper. Point out that if each of them had an infinitely large piece of paper and an infinite amount of time, the tree could go on forever. Talk together about how this is a tiny glimpse of eternity.

Creation hunt

Take a lesson to become hunters of the beauty of creation. Begin with a pentagon hunt, looking for things with five sides or parts (apples or pear, fruit and vegetables, starfish, sand dollar, some seashells). Move onto six-sided shapes such as honeycombs, the skin of a pineapple, kernels on corn on the cob. And then move to spirals such as seashells, horns on sheep, some tree trunks, some spider webs, a growing fern, a galaxy of stars, and more. See what the children come up with, and end the session talking about the beauty of creation and how we are called to be creators.

Quilt stories

Make a quilt throughout the year concerning the general theme of the year. Have each child design a quilt square that will show people what the theme is. The quilts can be made with material or foam or paint and paper. Choose what is going to work for your situation. Assemble the quilt as a group, and display it for all the children in all the religious education classes.

Good deed puzzle

Have each of the students make a good deed puzzle by giving them a piece of heavy paper. They need to draw the picture for the puzzle first. Pick out something that shows what we are called to do in service to another. Color the picture or paint it—whatever works. Then draw the puzzle piece shapes, and then cut them out. Assemble all the pieces in a container, and give to each other to solve. This exercise is readily adaptable for all age groups, and the puzzles can be as simple or as complex as needed.

Create counting rhymes

When there are specific things to learn, create a counting rhyme with a strong beat, repeating the same words over and over. Or use rhyme at the end of lines, finishing perhaps with a surprise. Another possibility is to use the same sounds over and over. Other variations would include a strong rhythm, a few numbers, or names of people.

Rhythm instruments

Easy to create rhythm instruments include jars with a different amount of water in each, spoons in one hand with the curved bowls together, which are slapped on the thigh in a rhythm, pop bottles with varying amounts of water and blowing across the tops, beans or other small object placed inside a small can or plastic container. Use these instruments to create songs and rhythms that add to the theme of the class.

This touches only the tip of the iceberg of intelligences. If we are open to our creative selves, we will be able to develop many opportunities for the intelligences to be alive in our community's faith life. Trust the Spirit, trust yourself, and trust the children you work with. Together you make faith an ever-vibrant force in our world.

TWELVE STEPS
AND SCRIPTURAL REFERENCES

THE TWELVE STEPS

We admitted we were powerless over alcohol, drugs, sex, food, etc. and that our lives had become unmanageable.

We came to believe that a Power greater than ourselves could restore us to sanity.

We made a decision to turn our will and our lives over to the care of God as we understood God.

We made a searching and fearless moral inventory of ourselves.

We admitted to God, to ourselves, and to another human being the exact nature of our wrongs.

We were entirely ready to have God remove all these defects of character.

We humbly asked God to remove our shortcomings.

We made a list of all persons we had harmed and became willing to make amends to them all.

We made direct amends to such people wherever possible, except when to do so would injure them or others.

We continued to take personal inventory and when we were wrong promptly admitted it.

We sought through prayer and meditation to improve our conscious contact with God, as we understood God, praying only for knowledge of God's will for us and the power to carry that out.

Having had a spiritual awakening as the result of these steps, we tried to carry this message to those addicted to something and to practice these principles in all our affairs.

Scriptural References

STEP ONE
"My spirit is broken, my lamp of life extinguished, and my burial is at hand. My days are passed away and my plans are at an end" (Job 17:1, 11).

STEP TWO
"Jesus said to him, 'If you can! Everything is possible to one who has faith.' Then the boy's father cried out, 'I do believe, help my unbelief!'" (Mark 9:23-24).

STEP THREE

"We have come to know and to believe in the love God has for us" (1 John 4:16).

STEP FOUR

"I give you a new commandment: love one another. As I have loved you, so you also should love one another. This is how all will know that you are my disciples, if you have love for one another" (John 13:34-35).

STEP FIVE

"I shall get up and go to my father and I shall say to him, 'Father, I have sinned against heaven and against you. I no longer deserve to be called your son...'" (Luke 15:18-19).

STEP SIX

"Save me, O God, for the waters threaten my life; I am sunk in the abysmal swamp where there is no foothold; I have reached the watery depths; the flood overwhelms me" (Psalm 69:2-3).

STEP SEVEN

"Christ Jesus did not regard equality with God something to be grasped. Rather, he emptied himself, taking the form of a slave...he humbled himself, becoming obedient to death, even death on a cross" (Philippians 2:5-8).

STEP EIGHT

"There is nothing concealed that will not be revealed, nor secret that will not be known. Therefore whatever you have said in the darkness will be heard in the light, and what you have whispered behind closed doors will be proclaimed on the housetops" (Luke 12:2-3).

STEP NINE

"But if we walk in the light as he is in the light, then we have fellowship with one another" (1 John 1:7).

STEP TEN

"I am bound, O God, by vows to you; your thank offerings I will fulfill. For you have rescued me from death, my feet, too, from stumbling; that I may walk before God in the light of the living" (Psalm 56:13-14).

STEP ELEVEN

"Know that I am with you; I will protect you wherever you go, and bring you back to this land. I will never leave you until I have done what I promised you" (Genesis 28:15).

STEP TWELVE

"Then I heard the voice of the Lord saying, 'Whom shall I send? Who will go for us?' 'Here I am,' I said. 'Send me!'" (Isaiah 6:8).

OTHER BOOKS BY
BERNADETTE STANKARD

Co-Creators with God
Creative Strategies for Faith Formation

Using anecdotes, practical advice, and theological insights, Bernadette talks about obstacles to creativity, creativity and faith formation, creativity in the spiritual life, transformation, the journey to wholeness, and sharing in God's creation.

128 PP | $14.95 | 978-1-58595-584-8

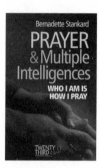

Prayer & Multiple Intelligences
Who I Am Is How I Pray

In clear, insightful prose, rich with real-life examples, this book discusses multiple intelligences and how they enable us to pray "as we are" and so develop a deeper friendship and intimacy with the God whose love transforms us.   **120 PP | $12.95 | 978-1-58595-512-1**

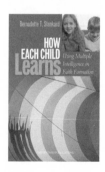

How Each Child Learns
Using Multiple Intellegence in Faith Formation

In this very lively book, Bernadette shows how the theory of multiple intelligence can be used to creatively teach religion to children. With concise and perceptive writing, she makes clear the benefits of using this approach in the classroom, home, and parish.   **120 PP | $14.95 | 978-1-58595-269-4**

1-800-321-0411
www.23rdpublications.com

TWENTY
THIRD
PUBLICATIONS